# THE NEW ART OF NEGOTIATING

## HOW TO CLOSE ANY DEAL

## GERARD I. NIERENBERG
## HENRY H. CALERO

SQUAREONE
PUBLISHERS

COVER DESIGNER: Jeannie Tudor
EDITOR: Helene Ciaravino
IN-HOUSE EDITOR: Michele D'Altorio
TYPESETTER: Gary A. Rosenberg

**Square One Publishers**
115 Herricks Road
Garden City Park, NY 11040
(516) 535-2010 • (877) 900-BOOK
www.squareonepublishers.com

**Library of Congress Cataloging-in-Publication Data**

Nierenberg, Gerard I.
  The new art of negotiating : how to close any deal / Gerard Nierenberg, Henry
H. Calero.
    p. cm.
  Rev. ed. of: The art of negotiating / Gerard I. Nierenberg. 1981.
  Includes index.
  ISBN 978-0-7570-0305-9
  1. Negotiation. I. Calero, Henry H. II. Nierenberg, Gerard I. Art of
negotiating. III. Title.
  BF637.N4N5 2009
  158'.5—dc22
                                2008049299

Printed in the United States of America

10   9   8   7   6   5   4   3   2   1

# Contents

*"Let us begin anew, remembering on both
sides that civility is not a sign of weakness.
That sincerity is always subject to proof.
Let us never negotiate out of fear,
but let us never fear to negotiate."*

—JOHN F. KENNEDY

# Preface

Information on the art of negotiating is totally lacking in many segments of society, especially in our educational system, which spends little (if any) time teaching how important negotiating skills will be in students' lives. As a result, many students leave learning institutions knowing a great deal about the arts, medicine, science, mathematics, engineering, and many other subjects, but they have little knowledge and understanding of how to conduct a negotiation in a respectful, persuasive, fruitful manner. Both of us came to this conclusion independently, but we found each other and pooled our resources so that we could bring texts and seminars on negotiating to the public and thus fill the need. Please allow us to explain how we came to work together and co-author *The New Art of Negotiating*.

In the early 1960s, Jerry was enjoying a highly successful career as an attorney on the East coast. He decided to put into print some of his best advice on negotiating, as the subject was not previously written on. So Jerry wrote *The Art of Negotiating*, which became a bestseller.

Meanwhile, Hank was successfully negotiating major contracts for an aerospace firm. At lunch one day, Hank's co-worker asked him where he had learned to negotiate. Hank couldn't answer that question, for he had never attended a university course or read a book on the subject. After all, such courses and texts were not available to him. That's when Hank realized the great need for guidance in the field of negotiation. In one week, Hank left his job with the aerospace industry and opened his own consulting firm. In fact, his former employer was his first client.

Ultimately, Hank developed a successful business on the West coast, conducting seminars on negotiating. He also kept abreast of new developments in the field. On a Sunday morning, while reading the *LA Times*, Hank saw that someone had actually written a book on the skills and techniques involved with negotiating. It was Jerry, of course. Hank immediately contacted Jerry.

After sharing stories about our individual seminars and work, we decided to pool our resources and talents. And the rest is history. We have been brainstorming, writing, speaking, and "work-shopping" together for decades now. Our comprehensive approach to the art of negotiating has proven to be an extremely effective tool. We are so excited to share our knowledge and experience with you.

We previously co-authored two other books, *How to Read a Person Like a Book* in 1971, and *MetaTalk* in 1973. The first book has sold more than 2 million copies and is still in print. Besides those two publications, we separately have written numerous other works. This revision covers what Jerry wrote in his original *The Art of Negotiating*, what Hank has written in his three books on negotiating, and what both of us learned from many years of conducting worldwide business.

It has been a true pleasure and adventure working with each other on the stimulating, exciting field of negotiating. We wish you the best in your own career and hope that we can, in some small way, assist you in becoming the negotiator you have always dreamed of being. Like any other art, negotiating involves natural talents but also well-applied dedication and practice. We're here to guide and support you—bolster high standards, encourage optimistic approaches, and aid you in fulfilling your greatest expectations.

# A Note on Gender

In the writing of our book, we were determined to fairly reference both male and female negotiators. In general, when a third-person pronoun is necessary, it is unbiased and conscientious to use "he or she" and "his or her." But that phrasing can be lengthy and awkward when employed repeatedly throughout paragraphs. So we decided to alternate gendered personal pronouns according to chapter. The odd-numbered chapters use masculine pronouns, while the even-numbered chapters use feminine pronouns. We hope this makes the writing both respectful and easy to read.

# The New Art of Negotiating

# Introduction

*"Negotiating in the classic diplomatic sense assumes*
*parties more anxious to agree than disagree."*
—DEAN ACHESON

N early every day of our lives—and, no doubt, your life, too—
has involved some sort of negotiation, major or minor. We
have long seen ourselves as problem-solvers. And from the
moment we realized that every negotiation involves problem-solving, we have seen ourselves as negotiators, too. We believe that
every obstacle that hinders negotiation, every issue of contention, is
merely a problem that needs to be solved. And the best way to solve
such problems, or negotiating issues, is to get all involved parties
working together toward an "everybody wins" solution.

That cooperative spirit is one of the first fundamentals we high-
light in *The New Art of Negotiating*. In Chapter 1, we introduce you to
the way we understand and define "negotiation"—what characterizes that term. And approaching a negotiation not as a game but as
a cooperative process or enterprise is a key concept. Chapter 2 is
also important for a solid background on negotiating; it discusses
why humans, in general, have a tendency to negotiate, and therefore
why the skills of negotiating are so important to our species. With
that solid background accomplished, we enter into a more detailed
study of how to conduct a negotiation.

While you're polishing your understanding of what it means to negotiate, why not polish your personal presentation? Chapter 3 brings us into the specifics, scrutinizing what makes a successful negotiator just that—from important skills to winning personality characteristics. Now what about the actual negotiation? It should start with great preparation. So Chapter 4 walks you through a step-by-step preparation agenda. That's followed by Chapter 5's discussion of effective techniques to use once the negotiation is underway. Included in that chapter is significant advice on how to break an impasse and how to avoid damaging assumptions.

If you are part of a negotiating team, then Chapter 6 is definitely for you. It analyzes the role of the chief negotiator or manager and then offers a section on team dynamics. Chapter 7 continues the focus on dealing with others, but delves into the psychology of how to read other people. This entertaining part of the book investigates such things as facial expressions, sounds and silence, gestures, and even gender tendencies. And finally, Chapter 8 gives you a few last words of advice, dispelling certain misconceptions that might prevent you from being the best negotiator you can be, and suggesting a battery of questions to ask as you perform a self-assessment of your work.

The material in this book has been gathered from our shared professional experiences and from the many seminars on negotiating that we have conducted over several decades. Everything we recommend has been tested by real people, including ourselves, and has proven effective. Throughout the chapters, we use quite a collection of humorous anecdotes and helpful examples. After all, we want you to enjoy the journey to becoming a successful negotiator. Take what you can from the pages of this book, and use it well. We applaud you for taking the step to developing more persuasive, more powerful, more artful negotiation skills.

# 1

# The Fundamentals of Negotiating

## A Starting Point

*"If you can't go around it, over it, or through it,
you had better negotiate with it."*

—ASHLEIGH BRILLIANT

There are few things in life that are simpler in definition yet broader in scope than negotiating. Every single desire demands some form of satisfaction, and every need seeks to be fulfilled. Whenever people exchange ideas with the intention of changing relationships to fulfill needs, they are negotiating. Whenever they confer for agreement, they are negotiating.

Negotiations are necessary in countless circumstances and in all areas of life. Think of a typical, seemingly straightforward occurrence: a salesman tries to close a deal. That sounds simple enough, right? Better yet, basically the proposition he has made is acceptable to the prospective customer. However, there are still a number of questions that need to be answered. How much discount will the salesman give? Who will store the bulk of the order—the buyer or the seller? Can the delivery date be improved in any way? Will the salesman agree to give the buyer additional price consideration and protection on reorders for two additional years? Both buyer and seller have to carefully negotiate these and many other matters. The task is quite complex.

To date, there have been no general theories available that can guide an individual in his day-to-day negotiating activities. There is no public school that teaches the students how to negotiate the daily compromises that life demands. Moreover, many students go through all four years of college without any educational exposure to the art of negotiating. All too frequently we are stuck learning to negotiate by trial and error. And that means that many of our negotiation tactics will be and are based on unique and very specific personal experiences. That doesn't mean, however, that you can't now learn a few skills that will help you be more constructive and prepared when it comes to negotiating. And this book will help you do so.

In this chapter, we will more thoroughly explore what negotiating actually is. Moreover, we will offer several fundamental approaches to negotiating, from adopting a cooperative perspective to keeping your emotions in control. These basics will organize your thoughts and prepare you for the more in-depth chapters to follow. So let's begin our adventure into the world of negotiating.

## CONSIDERING HOW OFTEN WE NEGOTIATE

Negotiation skills are only becoming more needed. Sure, the computer age has made many jobs obsolete. Yet the role of the negotiator has grown in importance. After all, the modern world is a place of instant connections, constant business, and proactive networking. Technology simply has provided us with more venues through which to negotiate—e-mail, voice mail, fax, text messages, remote video, and more.

And despite all of the wonderful technological advances that have been accomplished, we still are unable to negotiate with machines, including computers. The man-machine relationship is a physical one for accomplishing specific tasks or inputting and storing information; it is not for discussing mutual problems and resolving them. For example, one might argue that the Internet is now serving as a matchmaker and therefore affecting the very personal tradition of marriage, which is a classic negotiation situation. Yet even when a computer is used to serve as a matchmaker, the computer is merely predicting that perhaps two individual negotiators might have a chance of reaching a satisfactory agreement and relationship. The ultimate agreement has to come from the people directly involved.

So negotiating in the professional and the personal arenas is not a thing of the past. The art of negotiating is dynamic, vibrant, and so very needed. Every day, *The New York Times* reports hundreds of negotiations. At the United Nations and in national capitols around the world attempts are made to settle a variety of disputes. Government agencies negotiate with the United States Congress for appropriations—for example, a utility company confers with a regulatory agency on rates. An existing labor dispute is negotiated and settled. Two separate companies agree to merge but must obtain the consent of the Justice Department. A large or small piece of real estate changes hands. These are just a few of the types of negotiations that the newspapers around the nation describe on a daily basis. But even more important, at least to the individuals involved in them, are the countless negotiations that are not mentioned in *The New York Times* or any other newspaper.

Consider how many negotiations occur in your home and personal life each day, whether you're trying to keep the peace among siblings, decide on a dinner entrée, or select a paint color for the bedroom walls. A perfect example is found in the story of a father who heard his two teen-aged sons loudly arguing about which one of them was going to eat the last piece of leftover apple pie. Neither one of them would agree to an even split. The father wisely decided he would teach them something about negotiating. He suggested that one of them should cut the piece of pie into two segments, and then the other should make the first selection. It doesn't take a genius to figure out how the son holding the knife cut the pie—straight down the middle so that each one would wind up with an equal slice. The father taught the boys a valuable lesson in negotiating effectively and in satisfying needs. And he did so through a very ordinary situation. All of us regularly face such ordinary situations; all of us are negotiators on a daily basis.

# POSING NO LIMITS ON WHAT'S NEGOTIABLE

Because the word *negotiation* can cover so many events and situations, it is difficult to concisely define. The following passage is an excerpt from a study conducted by the Committee for the Judiciary of the U.S. Senate. It attempts to define what a negotiation is and what sets it up for success.

> Negotiation may be exploratory and serve to formulate viewpoints and delineate areas of agreement or contention. Or it may aim at working out practical arrangements. The success of negotiation depends on whether (a) the issue is negotiable (that is, you can sell your car, but not your child); (b) the negotiators interested not only in taking but also in giving are able to exchange value for value, and are willing to compromise; or (c) negotiating parties trust each other to some extent—if they didn't, a plethora of safety provisions would render the "agreement" workable.

The Committee's initial definition is broad and therefore hard to argue. But problems arise when we study the prerequisites for success that follow. Look once more at the first suggested condition for success. In truth, children *are* sold, even in America—as the occasional revelation of a black market baby ring clearly indicates. *All* issues must be considered negotiable whenever there are human needs to be met. Why put limits on what's negotiable?

As for the second condition mentioned, it is impossible to foresee in any negotiation what the outcome is going to be. Therefore, it is impossible to anticipate in advance that either party will be "willing to compromise." Compromise is usually arrived at during the normal course of bargaining. It develops naturally as a result of a thorough examination of the facts and common interests of the negotiators involved. Although compromises may be worked out as a result of the negotiation, the parties should not enter into discussion with the *sole* intent of compromising. An old saying is very applicable: "The wheels of diplomacy often run on the grease of ambiguity." It is better to enter into a negotiation without self-imposed limitations, ready to seize any advantage that is offered.

The committee's third stipulation is also unreliable. Often the parties involved in a negotiation do not trust each other. As an extreme example, a parent whose child is kidnapped would not hesitate to negotiate for his release; in such a situation, the parties certainly don't trust each other. And indeed, the handling of other people's mistrust is the skilled negotiator's stock in trade.

What is important to realize is that *every* situation involving human needs should be considered negotiable to some extent. So instead of trying to narrow down what situations are prime for negotiating and when negotiation strategies should be applied, let's be courageous and assume all situations are ripe for negotiating. And all of the fundamentals of negotiations offered hereafter can apply to the events of both your daily personal life and your professional life.

## UNDERSTANDING THE DIFFERENCE BETWEEN DEBATING AND NEGOTIATING

Let's assume that negotiating involves the giving and taking of words. That does not mean the negotiating parties need to begin on opposite sides of the ring and dive in for a verbal boxing match. A negotiation is not synonymous with a heated debate. Although it is impossible to negotiate without a certain amount of debating, effective negotiators understand the fundamental differences between the two. They debate when they want to and negotiate whenever it is appropriate and beneficial to do so. Further defining both terms will help distinguish them from each other.

To begin with, formal debating is governed by many rules. One of them limits the time for which a person may speak; in a debate, a person has a strictly limited amount of time to present his views, opinions, knowledge, and judgments. In contrast, negotiations are not so limited in the amount of time available to conclude them. They end only when a settlement has been reached, when conferencing is adjourned for another time, or when the efforts to negotiate are called off because of no settlement.

Another difference is that in a debate only one person or party can win. It is a contest conducted for purposes of producing a winner or winning side. However, in a negotiation it is possible for all those who participate to win.

Perhaps the most important difference between debating and negotiating involves the making of concessions and compromises. Quite simply, an experienced debater would never do so. Yet every negotiator knows that concessions and compromises are the fuel that drives the engine of negotiating. Without them, there would never be any agreement or settlement.

Moreover, debaters and negotiators differ in how they listen. The successful debater primarily listens for purposes of developing rebuttal, voicing a disagreement, or undermining what the other person has stated. The successful negotiator listens for those same purposes plus many others. For example, he listens for "needs" (since he has already heard "wants"); areas of possible compromise; disclosures; financial information; and the attitudes, feelings, and doubts of the other party.

And a negotiator also does something else a debater might not do: he asks many questions. Some of the questions are prepared beforehand, and others are asked extemporaneously. Questions allow the negotiator to gather information, understand various perspectives, acquire knowledge, and find solutions during the course of a negotiation.

We have spent more than thirty years leading seminars at which we record case-study, role-played negotiations on videotape. It has become very clear that, in these practice negotiations, the majority of time is spent debating instead of negotiating. It isn't until after the role-playing is done and the seminar attendees see the videotapes that they realize this fact. In the real world of negotiating, debating should be only a small part of the process, and that is what we suggest as one of the fundamentals of the art of negotiation.

## REDEFINING NEGOTIATING AS A COOPERATIVE ENTERPRISE

The process of negotiating has often been equated to a game. But a game has definite rules and a known set of values. Each player is limited in the moves he can make and the things he can and cannot do. In contrast, a negotiation is not subject to such specific rules of conduct. Conduct is controlled only by the personal and/or professional standards that the parties bring to the table.

Moreover, in a game, the risks and possible rewards are clearly known. In a negotiation, any risks that are known have been learned from experience, not a rule book or instruction sheet. Further, situations faced by a negotiator are variable; the negotiator often has no control over or pre-knowledge of the specific steps that will unfold.

So negotiation, in its purest sense, is a process—not a game. It is much more productive to think of negotiating as a *cooperative enterprise* into which the parties enter for the purpose of having needs, goals, and objectives satisfied. If both parties enter into a negotiation on a cooperative basis, there is a strong likelihood they will both strive for resolution. Certain goals will be shared. This does not mean that every goal will be of the same value to the participants. However, it does mean that there is greater possibility for each participant to reach his goals and satisfy his respective needs.

In summary, to view a negotiation as a game is to enter it predominantly in a competitive spirit, instead of having a cooperative or problem-solving attitude. The agenda of all games that pit individuals against each other is to wind up with winners and losers. The ultimate goal and objective in a negotiation should be to have everyone win—to have all involved wind up getting something they not only wanted, but also needed. Both parties must feel that they gained something.

In order to become successful in negotiating, the negotiators should have a sincere belief that, no matter how great the gulf between the parties, it will be possible to cross that gulf and join hands in a mutually satisfying conclusion. Yet a negotiation is also a cooperative *challenge*. We don't want to completely remove the competitive spirit! Negotiating will certainly cause you to flex your mind's muscles, and for most negotiators, that's the appeal of the whole deal. Successful negotiators know there will be times when they don't have "all the marbles," and they like it that way. After all, if they have all the aces in hand, no expertise is required to win. It takes a pro to know how to handle being on the short end of the stick. So the challenge is what makes negotiating an interesting task.

We have met some negotiators who state they actually enjoy bargaining from the underdog position because it forces them to use all of their skills and abilities. They can be compared with a baseball player in the late innings of a game, when his team is behind in the score. That player revels under the pressure of getting a base hit with bases loaded and winning the game.

So in effective negotiating, the underlying competitive attitude is not abandoned. Instead, it acts as an integrating element—a rivalry that coordinates and does not separate individuals. A single side of the scissors by itself cannot cut a piece of paper; it needs a complimentary side. Together the two sides create friction, which is necessary to build a bridge and produce results.

Former U.S. President Franklin D. Roosevelt once stated, "It has always seemed to me that the best symbol of common sense was a bridge." A great comedian, Robert Benchley, added, "It seems to me that the most difficult part of building a bridge would be the start." Benchley's statement is very important because what we must listen and look for early in a negotiation are comments and statements that reveal possible common interests and needs. Such areas may turn out to be wonderful spots to lay the foundation and take the first step in constructing the bridge between you and the other party.

A classic example of creating a climate for overcoming differences is found in what Queen Elizabeth II said in West Germany shortly after the end of World War II: "For fifty years we heard too much about the things which divided us. Let us now make a great effort to remember the things which unite us. With these links, we can begin to forge a new and better understanding of the future." Here are a few more examples of how the cooperative approach can wield a successful negotiation, and how a one-sided approach can doom a negotiation.

## A Ride on the Radio Waves

Jerry remembers a time when he, as an attorney, was representing a trade association of radio and television servicemen. At one of the association meetings, the members were brainstorming about how to more effectively attract new members, and also how to do more for the existing members. The major focus was on how to get necessary publicity.

It seemed logical to get the cause on radio, since the members serviced radios. In a very short time they came up with a highly creative and cooperative idea. It was the old "you scratch my back and I'll scratch yours" negotiation strategy. They offered the radio stations a proposal: in return for free publicity on the air, the servicemen would advertise the name of the radio station in their store windows. They would also make sure the station was properly received on every set they repaired. This cooperative agreement worked to perfection.

## A "Higher" Plan for Church Property

Compromise—working together toward a solution—helped bring St. Peter's Church and Citicorp together for their mutual benefit. Jerry had, for many years, helped the St. Peter's Church, which is located at Lexington Avenue and 53rd Street in the City of New York. The location is a prime piece of real estate. One afternoon, Reverend Peterson, then the pastor of the church, shared with Jerry the news that Citicorp had approached him with a substantial offer to buy both the church and its land. Reverend Peterson had consulted with both the church board and his neighbors, and everyone united in opposition to the sale. The landmark church was a fixture in the neighborhood, and no one wanted to see it replaced with a high-rise office building.

Yet despite this opposition, Reverend Peterson did not want to turn Citicorp down flat. Even if it meant finding a new location and building a new church, the pastor felt certain that the church could make good use of the astronomical amount of money Citicorp was offering. Reverend Peterson asked if Jerry, as a professional negotiator, had any advice or suggestions that might help him in this situation.

Jerry's professional experience working with railroad companies—building on and over railroad properties—gave him an idea. Instead of tearing down the church to construct an office tower, why not allow Citicorp to build over the church? The corporation would rent what was then "air space" and literally build a structure that sat above the church, leaving the original building as it was.

If everybody agreed on this solution, it could benefit all of the involved parties. St. Peter's could continue to operate without inter-ruption—something the church could not do if it sold the building and land outright. In fact, with the money paid by Citicorp, the church could renovate the entire first floor of the building, improv-ing both the facilities and the services it offered its worshippers. These were improvements the church could not afford if it turned down Citicorp's offer outright. Meanwhile, Citicorp would gain a central Manhattan location for its offices, and by becoming tenants, would do so at less cost than buying the property.

Both the church board and Citicorp found this approach very appealing. Citicorp agreed to pay a sum that would completely cover the ground-floor renovations of the church, and more. After obtaining estimates on the cost of construction from contractors, the board of St. Peter's and Citicorp settled on an amount and wrote it into the contract. As in all truly successful negotiations, the parties found a solution in which everybody wins!

Well, everybody but the Reverend Peterson. As an unrelated but interesting aside, the reverend—for reasons of his own—waited nearly two years after concluding the deal with Citicorp before let-ting out the contract for construction on the church. Unfortunately, during those boom years of Manhattan construction, the cost of the renovations skyrocketed above the original estimates. By then, the contracts exceeded the amount Citicorp had paid St. Peter's by sev-eral million dollars. The church found itself in the position of having to ask its parishioners for funds or cut back on the renovations. And the Reverend Peterson found himself out of a job.

## A Lesson on Team Spirit

An overwhelmingly one-sided settlement breeds trouble and, in the end, will only prove to be a great waste of time and effort. Some negotiators who are intensely competitive wonder why they can't seem to conclude certain deals. They like to remark that they work hard, but somehow luck and life never seem to give them any breaks, that something always goes wrong for them. Apparently such people haven't yet discovered that life is one massive cooperative experience. We would be able to complete few tasks without the help, assistance, and cooperation of others. Here's an example of a general manager who learned this lesson the hard way.

A few years ago, a well-known professional athlete wanted more money in his yearly contract. For several reasons he had attempted to do his own negotiating with management, and he failed to reach a satisfactory settlement. Although the athlete had considerable wealth and intelligence, he was very shy and, by his own admission, "no match negotiating with the general manager." The athlete's assessment turned out to be correct, because the general manager (GM) had an ace up his sleeve: a reserve clause in the contract that made it impossible for the athlete to move from one team to another. As a result of this, the general manager wanted the player to sign for less than he deserved. Becoming aware of these details, the athlete became so demoralized that he conducted subsequent negotiations by letter, instead of in person.

That's when an agent suggested to the athlete that, although the reserve clause prohibited him from playing for another team, there was nothing in the contract that would keep him from dropping out of sports. Despite the athlete's shyness, he had a very pleasant personality and was handsome. Other individuals with much less presence had previously established careers in show business, so why shouldn't this attractive man do so? Negotiations began with an independent film producer. In a short time, there developed the prospect of a five-year contract with that producer.

Suddenly the pressure was on the GM. If the athlete signed with the film producer and left the sports team, the sports fans would react adversely. The team would suffer at the box office and the owners would become very upset with the GM. In short, his job was on the line.

As a result of all of this, the athlete received an enormous increase in his salary, and the other members of the team used the same strategy in their contract negotiations. The moral of the story is quite simple: never press for a deal that is beneficial solely to your side and comes at the expense of everyone else involved. The GM learned the hard way that negotiating should be a cooperative enterprise. The poet Edna St.Vincent Millay observed, "Even the lowly rat in adversity has courage to turn and fight." If the general manager had been willing to negotiate in a cooperative spirit, instead of initially attempting to dominate the athlete, he would have eliminated wasted time, avoided problems, and saved management a great deal of money in salaries.

## A Blotch in the Ink

Here's another example of how *not* to negotiate. Many years ago in New York City, the individual who was head of the printers' union became known as someone who "drives a hard bargain." He lead the printers in several paralyzing union strikes, and he ultimately achieved the goal of obtaining remarkable contract settlements. Not only did the printers obtain higher wages, but also the newspapers were forbidden to institute such money-saving practices as the automated setting of market tables. The printers won their points at the negotiating table because they held out to the end. Looks like success, right?

But the printers' union didn't look at the bigger picture. The newspapers were forced into an economic straightjacket. Three major newspapers merged and, finally, after another long strike, folded. New York City was left with only one evening and two morning newspapers. And that left thousands and thousands of newspaper employees—including printers—without jobs. Thus, to use a metaphor, while the operation was very successful, the patient ultimately died. The printers union did not foresee that a sweeping one-sided victory often does not produce long-term advantages for the supposed winner.

There is great success associated with the cooperative approach to negotiating. If you and I exchange ideas, where each of us had one idea we now have two. And no one has lost anything. In life it is possible to make others wealthier without going broke and penniless ourselves. This principle is precisely what the cooperative process is in a negotiation.

Some negotiations conducted in a highly competitive and aggressive manner end in what appears to be a tremendous win for one side. However, such endings are seldom accepted as settled. The reason is obvious, for unless the terms and conditions arrived at are somehow advantageous to the "loser," the losing party will soon seek ways and means of changing the settlement reached. During our negotiating seminars we have often asked the attendees, "Have you ever *really* won an argument with your spouse?"

Unlike a game in which a clear winner is decided at the end, negotiations don't have such clear-cut conclusions. They don't end when you walk away from the table, and in some instances that's when the real negotiations begin. This is especially true in a divorce settlement negotiation. If one of the parties believes he came out on the short end of the stick, look out—it's going to be a very rocky road in the weeks, months, and years that follow.

In order to get both sides working together, the skilled negotiator needs to find common ground that will motivate both sides to cooperate in finding solutions. In many cases, the negotiator can find common ground by helping both sides realize that "making more pie" will benefit everyone; allowing everybody to have a bigger share of pie is much more rewarding than fighting over the last remaining piece. Of course, this approach often requires creative thinking aimed at coming up with previously unimagined solutions—such as the solution Jerry devised in the story involving St. Peter's Church. But finding common ground almost always produces better results and paves the way for future benefits by creating solid working or personal relationships.

## KEEPING EGOS AND EMOTIONS ON THE LOW

We have both participated in thousands of negotiations, and neither of us can recall two that were alike. Not only were the issues different, but so were the individuals. Therefore, it is dangerous to plan a forthcoming negotiation based on the conduct that arose in the last one; we can learn from the past, but history never quite repeats itself. An attendee at one of our seminars said, "The most important thing I've learned in all the years I've been negotiating is,

'Different strokes for different folks!'" We could not possibly improve on that statement.

All of the negotiations you will ever be involved in have three, and only three, fundamental things in common. First, people tell you what they *want* and not what they really *need.* Second, what you see and hear beyond the wants and needs will always be something different, often something unusual, and quite simply something that's extraneous. Finally, throughout the negotiating process each side will be listening and looking for any signs or clues that may provide a negotiating advantage. Each side will also be on a constant search to find out what the other side will accept.

It is always fascinating to observe two master negotiators battling it out. As a general rule, they usually are able to arrive at a settlement in a short time because they go directly to the heart of the problem and waste very little time. Each one—after an initial period of sparring, probing, and feeling out the other—promptly realizes that he is dealing with a master. Each can also estimate at what time a solution is likely to be forthcoming. They don't allow unnecessary "extras" to consume valuable time like so many others with less experience.

It must be stated that when two expert negotiators bargain in a calculated manner—like pro poker players—it is merely a surface-level view that we are witnessing. Underneath their calm exterior, there is a great amount of emotions. There are very few negotiations that proceed smoothly, without any difficult undercurrents. However, expert negotiators can control their emotions. They seldom do or say anything that may cause conflict or confrontation—especially at the beginning, when tensions are high. Instead, expert negotiators are extremely alert in observing any areas of possible compromise or common interest. Their principle interest at the outset is avoiding any pitfalls that may lead to conflict. And keeping emotions under wraps actually saves a lot of time.

Less experienced negotiators, in many instances, get into heated arguments very quickly. And usually those arguments revolve around very minor issues—even unimportant ones. Perhaps we might say that the pros keep their egos in check, whereas those with less experience often don't.

A person who attended one of our seminars once loudly stated, "I like to start my negotiations by getting opponents angry, frustrated, and off balance in their game!" The other attendees looked at Hank to discover what his response might be. Hank explained that in a *game* it certainly can be productive to do that, and sometimes it works well. And then he told of his experience as a high school baseball pitcher. He was labeled as a "head hunter," because in the early innings of a game, Hank always threw a few pitches at the batters' heads. He did this so that they would back away from the plate, which gave him an advantage for his outside curveball. But Hank reminded the group that he was playing a game, not conducting a negotiation. In negotiations, raw emotions and aggressive moves set tensions that could defeat any healthy, cooperative spirit that is present.

Most negotiations contain enough friction at the onset, so there is little benefit to creating more. At that early stage, each side conveys its position on the issues and usually its maximum goals, objectives, and demands. Again, it is worthwhile remembering that, at the beginning, negotiators will tell you what they want, and not what they need. And it is your job to narrow that distance between wants and needs by listening closely to what is said and asking questions designed to get the information you need. Believe it or not, a simple question that works really well is, "Now that you have told us what you *want,* what do you really *need*?" It is amazing how often people respond by saying, "What I really need is. . . ." And what they state is usually less than what they originally asked for. Keeping aggression and emotions in check will allow the other party to feel as though they can be sincere and straightforward.

Effective negotiating also requires developing self-control for the later parts of a negotiation. Frustrating situations and charged conditions often arise. And when the other party appears to be on the run, you might feel a great temptation to push them over the cliff. However, it you do that, you may wind up concluding a "lose-lose" negotiation that started out with such promise. You can look in a mirror and see who the cause for its failure was.

In simple terms, a negotiator must learn when to stop and when to shut up! He must work at controlling ego and emotions just as he works at controlling other habits that can be destructive, such as alcohol consumption, swearing, and the like. In some negotiations one word is as dangerous as "one more drink for the road." In many negotiations, there is a very critical point at which an improper reaction may blow things up altogether. Therefore, a great amount of caution should constantly be on your mind not to reach a point from which you cannot pull back and return to the norm. This is not easily accomplished, because in the heat of a negotiation we can get carried away, especially when the ego is in control and has taken over.

Jerry once retained a client who was the last tenant in an office building scheduled to be demolished. The new owner of the property planned to replace the four-story building with a skyscraper. All of the other tenants had moved out, but the aforementioned tenant still had two years left on his lease. The landlord wanted to get started on his new project immediately. Jerry's function, in addition to protecting his client's rights, was to work out a solution acceptable to both parties.

The landlord recognized that in order to get the tenant out of the building, he would have to pay money. It was how much money that concerned him. So he approached Jerry and asked, "How much do you want?" Jerry quickly replied, "You're the one who is buying. I'm not selling!" This placed the burden on the landlord.

The opening offer indicated the landlord's willingness to pay moving expenses. Jerry immediately declined it and asked for a cash offer instead. The landlord offered $25,000, and Jerry refused it. The landlord then walked out, mumbling something under his breath as he left the office.

In the days that followed, the landlord used delay as a tactic. However, this served to work against him because the tenant was in no hurry to vacate the premises. The landlord's next move consisted of having his attorney contact Jerry with a figure of $50,000, which was also turned down.

The subsequent offers became higher as Jerry did his homework, calculating what the landlord initially paid for the building, how much it might cost him to keep it vacant, and the cost involved in order to hold the mortgage commitments the landlord had made. And when his homework was completed, Jerry came up with a figure of a quarter of a million dollars. Not wanting to squeeze the landlord too hard, believing in the power of cooperation, Jerry cut the figure in half. The parties finally settled for $125,000.

Jerry learned that his "pushing hard but not too hard" approach truly paid off. When the landlord's attorney delivered the check to him, Jerry was advised that if he had asked for $5 more, a crane might have "accidentally" struck the building. The building would have then been declared a hazard that had to be torn down, and Jerry's client would have received nothing. Jerry's ability to bargain, not bully, produced a satisfying negotiation. His client benefitted from having a patient negotiator who kept ego and emotions under control. Jerry never reacted too quickly or too harshly.

## CONCLUSION

Master negotiators don't grow on trees and are indeed a rare commodity. A reason for this is that the art of negotiation truly involves a number of challenging fundamentals that can only be mastered by time, practice, and self-work. This chapter has summarized those fundamentals, including emphasis on cooperative spirit and control of emotions. Fred Charles Ikle, in his book *How Nations Negotiate,* has written, "The compleat negotiator, according to seventeenth and eighteenth century manuals on diplomacy, should have a quick mind but unlimited patience, know how to dissemble without being a liar, inspire trust without trusting others, be modest but assertive, charm others, without succumbing to their charm, and possess plenty of money and a beautiful wife while remaining indifferent to all temptation of riches and women."

There is a lot more to say about master negotiators. We will characterize the successful negotiator—his talents and traits—in Chapter 3. But first, let's look at human behavior in general. Chapter 2 will explore what it is about the human being that drives him toward negotiating. Read on for insights into yourself and others.

# 2

# Basic Human Behavior
## Needs, Patterns, and Motivation

*"The proper study of mankind is man!"*
—ALEXANDER POPE

The cooperative approach to negotiation—the approach that postulates that all parties must come away having gained something—is based on a very simple and important premise: whatever problems may exist, all negotiations are solved by mutual efforts. It therefore stands to reason that in order for an individual to successfully negotiate, she must have knowledge of people— for without it, she could not conduct productive mutual efforts. For those who are frequently negotiating in the professional arena, a solid understanding of basic human behavior is absolutely essential.

The manner and ways in which we learn about human behavior are as diverse and complex as the human being itself. We learn by reading, by listening, by observing, by finding out how people react or reacted in certain situations. Every newspaper story, every casual conversation, even every train and airplane trip gives us an opportunity to build upon our storehouse of information concerning human behavior.

Certainly use whatever events and situations present themselves in order to become a more educated student of human behavior. But in addition, consider the information we offer in this chapter. In the following sections we look at certain aspects of human behavior that pertain to the art of negotiating. Over the course of this chapter, we study people's most fundamental needs, as well as common behavior patterns, such as rationalization and role-playing, that can significantly affect how someone acts at the negotiating table. We also explore motivation in general—what drives a person to negotiate in the way she does. But first, let's try to answer a big question: is there *anything* predictable about human behavior, therefore allowing us to study it fruitfully at all?

## PREDICTING BEHAVIOR

According to Machiavelli, "Wise men say, and not without reason, that whoever wishes to foresee the future must consult the past; for human events ever resemble those of preceding times. This arises from the fact that they are produced by men who have been, and ever will be, animated by the same passions, and thus they must necessarily have the same results." In spite of the complexity of human behavior, in some instances it is predictable and understandable. The fields of history and psychology have taught us that much. In order to discover the predictable elements of human behavior, an intensive analysis is useful. Yet under certain conditions, such predictions become simple if we consider the actions of individuals as members of a large group of similar creatures.

As an example of this, when individuals firmly cross their arms, they are usually defensive. In many team negotiations, when one party is defensive, the majority of the members of that party will, in fact, have their arms crossed. When you serve as a negotiator often enough, certain patterns of behavior arise as common. It's kind of like the predictability based on mathematical laws. In any given number of coin tosses, the probability is that heads will come up 50 percent of the time and tails will come up 50 percent of the time.

Hank recalls a manager he worked for many years ago in the aerospace industry. In meetings, whenever the manager reached a point where his anger was about to boil over, he would reach for a pencil, pick it up, and start twisting it in his hands. And when the moment of eruption came, he would break the pencil in two, stand up, and give someone a serious tongue-lashing. Those who worked in that department became aware of the boss' behavior. Before a meeting, they would whisper to each other, "Watch out for the pencil!" That pencil-breaking is not unique to the one man under discussion; using force to break small, insignificant objects and thus relieve frustration is a very common human behavior.

It's very helpful to track clues like the pencil-twisting one. If an issue were being pressed or a deal were being forced, the twisting of the pencil would signal to a skilled negotiator that it is time to pull back a little, use a distraction tactic, or at least change the tone temporarily. If you still need convincing that human beings are indeed quite predictable, read the following additional examples.

## Weird Water Use

Predictability in human behavior is evident in a situation concerning the use of water in New York City. It was discovered that the water pressure began dropping off in the evening hours, exactly on the hour and the half-hour. The pressure drop was so precipitous and consistent that it caused great concern. The officials at the Water Department selected a random sample of the city's population that was large enough to give reliable results; they also subjected those people to psychologists, sociologists, mathematicians, and detectives.

The combined efforts resulted in a finding that between the hours of 7:00 PM and 10:00 PM, precisely on the hour and half-hour marks, toilets were being flushed and a corresponding number of water faucets were turned on. Ultimately, the reason for such behavior was very simple to explain. At those particular times, people who had been watching television would get up during the commercial breaks, go into the kitchen or bathroom, and run the water for their ordinary tasks.

## A Matter of Mah-Jong

On the other side of the world, the restaurant owners in Hong Kong have a very interesting way of negotiating with the city health inspectors—all based on human predictability. It is traditional for the city's health inspectors, after conducting an inspection of a restaurant, to drop into the back room at certain hours of the day to play the popular game of Mah-jong. And it can also be predicted that the inspectors will *always* win, because in the long history of that wonderful city, a city inspector has never lost any money.

If you were traveling in a train and it suddenly came to a stop, your thoughts most likely would be that a mechanical problem had occurred and not that the train stopped simply because the engineer wanted to pick some wildflowers along the tracks. In order words, you subconsciously acknowledge that the mechanical behavior of the train is less predictable than the human behavior of the engineer. As Sherlock Holmes explained to Dr. Watson, "While the individual man is an insoluble puzzle, in the aggregate, he becomes a mathematical certainty. You can never foretell what any one man will do, but you can always predict with precision what an average number of men will be up to. Individuals vary but percentages remain constant." It is unfortunate that many people involved in negotiations fail to utilize this type of working hypothesis as a convenient negotiating tool.

Jerry has sat down at the bargaining table on many occasions with lawyers, businessmen, and real estate operators. And for the most part, they proved to be reasonably skilled, resourceful negotiators, even though they may never have studied the fundamental elements of human behavior. Most of them relied on their personal experiences and the insights they gained from many years of bargaining. Unconsciously, they had acquired a great deal of knowledge, comprehension, wisdom, and skill in understanding people. And as the expression states, "You can't disagree with success." However, we both believe that those individuals are capable of even further increasing their awareness and abilities of other people, making that awareness conscious, by studying the elements of human behavior we will turn to in the next section. Doing so offers insight into the wide range of possibilities that are available in a negotiating situation.

After spending several paragraphs above on the predictability of human behavior, and before moving on, it is important to point out that there are always going to be exceptions. During life we make a great number of assumptions and judgments on how individuals will behave based on the how a great number of people have behaved in similar situations and conditions. But then there are the folks who throw us for a loop. For example, have you ever been in a gambling casino and noticed how many individuals will rub their hands together just before they receive a large amount of money that they have won at either a dice table or while playing roulette? Well, we once saw an elderly man who won thousands of dollars at a dice table and didn't flinch an inch. There was no change in his facial expression. Perhaps he was already a very wealthy man. Regardless, exceptions are not what we're interested in further covering here.

## LEARNING WHAT PEOPLE NEED

We have already established that people come to the negotiating table—or the kitchen table, where a lot of negotiating takes place—with needs that must be fulfilled. A skilled negotiator can swim through the wants and get to the basic needs of the other party, and then ultimately get that party to express which needs are most dire. Studying how people—and thus companies, organizations, and the like—unconsciously categorize their most basic needs will help you to become one of those skilled negotiators. Understanding the various types of needs gives us a useful framework for the understanding and awareness of an individual's conduct in a negotiation.

The subject of human needs has been studied by a number of people, but we find Abraham Maslow's work to be particularly compelling and applicable to the art of negotiating. Professor Maslow presents seven categories of universal human needs that greatly influence human behavior: physiological (homeostatic) needs; safety and security needs; the need for love and belonging; the need for esteem; the need for self-actualization; the need to know and understand; and aesthetic needs. Let's take a closer look at each of these families of needs.

## *Physiological (Homeostatic) Needs*

Physiological needs are common to all members of the animal kingdom. They are the needs for satisfaction of biological drives and urges such as hunger, fatigue, and sexual desire. Actually, the body makes automatic efforts to maintain itself at a normal and balanced state, called homeostasis. When the balance is off, the body cannot experience a sense of well-being. Strong needs develop that must be fulfilled in order for the body to get back to a balanced contentment. The answering of these needs allows us to exist.

Of all the seven families of needs, physiological needs are the most important. Without existence, all the other six don't matter at all. We need air, food, water, and rest. Homeostatic needs are the source of life itself. A person may lack love, safety, or esteem at times. Yet, if at the same time she is thirsty or hungry, her physiological needs far outweigh the others. An individual who is starving is surely not motivated to paint a picture or write a poem while her stomach is making all kinds of noise. For that person, no other interest exists except being fed; until she is, nothing else matters.

We must remember that our entire organism is involved whenever we have a specific need. Have you ever heard someone state, "My stomach is hungry?" Of course not; they say, "I'm hungry." Whenever someone is truly hungry, her whole being is involved and her perceptions change as a result. Her memory is affected, and the emotions are aroused by tensions and nervous feelings. Incidentally, when that need is finally satisfied, another one takes center stage and motivates the individual in another direction.

## *Safety and Security*

After our fundamental physiological needs are satisfied, our entire organism is then primarily concerned with our need for safety and comfort. The need colors our entire outlook and attitude in life. It may be observed in children more often than adults. The fundamental reason is simply because most adults have been taught to inhibit their overt reaction to any danger perceived.

A child will feel safe in a predictable and orderly environment—a place where there is a daily routine and no jarring surprises. Basically, a child desires to be in a place where she is protected from harm, usually by her parents. In contrast, adults are motivated to seek safety and security in such things as money in the bank, job security, and retirement programs. Although we no longer have to fear wild animals in a jungle, we need protection and security from the perils and dangers faced daily in economic competition. Note that we're really talking about the same type of need, and just looking at different ways to fill it.

## Love and Belonging

When the first two needs are satisfied, the third one always pops up. John Donne, a great writer and poet, once wrote, "No man is an island unto himself." He was, of course, speaking not just of men, but of women and children too. All humans innately have a strong need and craving for love and affection. We possess an inner longing for friends, acquaintances, even a sweetheart or someone with whom to intimately share our lives. And when the need is not satisfied, the drive may be so strong that the individual will go to any lengths to get it, sometimes displaying strange and unusual behavior.

It is a sad note that in our modern society, which offers countless creature comforts, there are so many people who have feelings of not being loved. Mother Teresa was a wonderfully caring individual who understood this need in India, where she lived. Because she had tremendous compassion for those who suffered great need for love, she spent many years of her life caring for and giving love to the homeless. She negotiated the dangerous streets of Bombay without any fear, performing her self-imposed duties on a daily basis.

## Esteem

The next need is our need for esteem, which may be seen in different dimensions. First and foremost, it is the need for independence and freedom. And an aspect of this is a need for strength of character, competence, and confidence in facing the world. Coupled with these is our desire for recognition from others and the prestige that accompanies it. Whenever a person senses fulfillment in these areas, she feels that she holds a useful and necessary place in the world.

While on the subject of esteem, there is an overwhelming amount of research that has been conducted that clearly illustrates the power of self-esteem as a source of motivation. It is like an engine driving a powerful train to its destination—literally unstoppable. Studies of individuals at various management levels reflect that feeling good about oneself is extremely important in accomplishing results and objectives at work. Research proves that the more this inner feeling exists, the greater that individual's competence and job performance will be.

When studying the motivation of salespeople, the Research Institute of America reached similar conclusions. Many individuals in sales believe self and social approval often motivates them and helps them to achieve greater effort and results. Most buyers are not aware of the pride salespeople have in making a sale. There is considerable respect from others in sales whenever a person is capable of making a sale to a tough customer. The kudos given to the successful salesperson is something seldom seen by a buyer.

## Self-Actualization

Now let's take the topic of motivation and persistence a step farther. Along with Maslow, we believe that every person, to some degree, is motivated to become self-actualized. In general terms, self-actualization is an inner desire and longing to reach the highest possible potential in what we do.

Think of a woman executive knowing she is capable of one day becoming the president of her company; she is self-actualized, understanding her strengths, desires, and vocation, and feeling comfortable and compelled enough to pursue them. Or consider a State Senator who has the inner knowledge and the ability to become President of the United States and actually realizes that goal. When we were both very young, we were self-actualized to the degree that we knew one day our names would be in print—and not for committing some illegal behavior or conduct. So self-actualization involves being courageous and introspective enough to study your own potential, grasp it, and then meet it.

## The Need to Know

There is a common need to seek out information, to explore and to understand. It is primarily curiosity that motivates us in finding answers to the many questions we have in life. This need is demonstrated by all of us at a very early age. When children begin to talk, the word *why* is constantly on their lips. Most parents run out of answers to their children's questions, mostly because they truly don't know the correct answers. So they attempt to quiet the child by saying, "Simply because."

Although it seems basic, people rarely think about the fact that the need to know, or the need to acquire knowledge, has been one the most important factors in the development of civilization and mankind. This is especially true in the creation and invention of modern things we take for granted, such as airplanes, automobiles, radio, television, and microwave ovens. It was curiosity and the need to know that motivated Sir Isaac Newton in discovering gravity—he had to find the answer to why an apple fell off a tree. His curiosity caused him to wonder, "Why didn't the apple fall upwards?" This need is best satisfied in a society where an individual's need to know and understand can be expressed and exercised. When this occurs, the spark of creativity is free to ignite and often leads to many inventions that, in turn, change the world.

## Aesthetics

And the last need on the totem pole of human needs involves the aesthetic. It is the appreciation of and desire for beauty in our world. Unfortunately, only a small segment of the population seeks to fulfill this need at a very strong level. That would be the artists, musicians, and others with similarly artistic lives. Maslow describes the aesthetic person as one who "feels a strong compulsion to straighten the crookedly hung picture on the wall."

Indeed, the need for order and balance is a basic part of all aesthetic expression. However, don't confuse the word *aesthetic* with being *fastidious*; a person who is fastidious is very difficult to please due to her high attention to detail. We're sure you have encountered both types of individuals during the course of your negotiating career.

We have presented the seven basic human needs in a descending order of importance. Most individuals would prioritize their needs in the order we have provided here. However, as Maslow has stated, "The order is not rigid and does not apply to all people." Undoubtedly, there are some to whom esteem is more important than love, just as some creative individuals hold aesthetic needs at great importance in their lives and therefore would not place them in the final spot on the list.

Why is it important to have an awareness of these fundamental needs? Well, with this greater awareness we can approach those with whom we negotiate with a newfound sensitivity and understanding. For example, when the other party is ruthlessly pursuing more money from your side, remember the explanation of security needs. Is that party panicking because its financial security seems flimsy? Or maybe the company's financial security is fine, but the particular negotiator is seeking a higher level of esteem within her company. Did you consider that her motivation in pursuing more money might be based on bettering her reputation? You will now start to ask more questions, and to see your fellow negotiators as human beings with the same needs as you. Both of those results will make you a better negotiator.

## APPLYING PSYCHOLOGY'S TERMS

We have just finished a rather in-depth discussion on needs. All of us experience various needs at any given moment, but wearing those needs on our sleeves can make us appear and/or feel vulnerable. So in true human fashion, most of us unconsciously mask those needs and present ourselves quite differently than we actually are.

Moreover, every individual has an image of herself that she synthesizes from her aspirations and experiences. Many personal decisions are made either to protect that self-image or to enhance it. Numerous behavioral patterns are geared toward this goal.

Our goal is to help you better understand individuals. The next step is to learn about standard types of behavior that psychologists have identified as common when people are presenting themselves to others, whether at a negotiation or other event. Once we understand these behaviors, we can better respond to and manage them—in ourselves and in others.

Again, a disclaimer is necessary. We have mentioned that negotiations are never exact repeats of previous ones, but that people, in general, are predictable to a certain degree. Even regarding behavioral patterns, however, there is always the possibility that a person you have "de-coded" might arrive at a clearer picture of her self-image by studying her previous actions and experiences and then changing. So even if we analyze a person and predict her behavior based on that displayed in past negotiations, we must accept that our predictions are not foolproof. Moreover, a lot of human behavior results from unconscious processes. Such behavior is not premeditated or intentional, which makes it difficult for us to predict and respond to perfectly.

## Rationalization

Whenever a person rationalizes, she is interpreting a situation in a manner that will place her in the most favorable position. Sometimes this means she will even convince herself of lies in order to make her behavior more agreeable to her own expectations and those of others. There is a character in *The Mikado,* a Gilbert and Sullivan operetta, who rationalizes a lie by calling it a "merely corroborative detail tended to give artistic verisimilitude to a bald and unconvincing narrative." It might be worthwhile remembering those words and humorously using them the next time you are caught red-handed telling a bald lie!

In order to avoid unpleasant feelings, bring about greater conformity, and remain in line with inner expectations, people often reconstruct past events in ways that make those events favorable, primarily to them only. They rationalize in order to justify their decisions, to vent their feelings, or perhaps to make themselves more acceptable to their peers. We often see such behavior in groups, organizations, or families in which a person tries to ascend the pecking order and place herself in a higher position.

It isn't unusual, at the conclusion of a negotiation, to hear someone rationalize her conduct, as well as the outcome or results. We are all probably familiar with the children's fable about the fox who was unable to reach and grasp a bunch of grapes. He rationalized by saying, "Oh well, they were probably sour and so I didn't really want them." He really wanted the grapes very badly, but he attempted to cover up his true feelings in order to feel and appear less desperate and less of a failure. Every reasoning person can probably recall one or more times at which she tried to rationalize something.

And there is another form of rationalization called *reverse sour grapes*. It occurs when people are rejected by an "in-group" and seek another means for revenge. There is a drive to prove oneself more capable than and ultimately superior to those who did the rejecting or winning. For example, a factory worker who is outcast by coworkers becomes a rate-buster and produces more than anyone else at the factory. In history, there have been many individuals who were driven by the same compulsion to "show them" and became very successful as a result.

# Projection

Projection occurs whenever a person assigns her motives to other individuals. This frequently occurs unconsciously. For example, Jerry was once authorized to negotiate the purchase of a motel chain for a client. In discussing the transaction, Jerry asked his client if he had ever used any outstanding negotiating techniques. The client's response was that he had used a technique of taking advantage of people's desire to make money. The client was ascribing to other people his own motivation of making money out of every negotiation. And the client's method had worked in the majority of cases because it was based on a fundamental human need. However, when it was used in the negotiation for the motel chain, it failed—and there was no settlement.

Projection is one of the most common and important ways humans perceive and think about objects in the external environment. The individual is usually unaware that she is distorting her outward perceptions by coloring them with her own characterization. Interestingly, people tend to project their undesirable traits and behavior, such as when a cheater uses self-consolation by reflecting that everyone cheats. Or as Bernard Shaw once remarked, "The chief punishment of a liar is that he cannot believe others."

## Displacement

Displacement happens when individuals vent anger or take out their aggression on a person or object that is not the cause of their difficulty. They seek a scapegoat. This is typical of a husband who comes home from work loaded with suppressed emotions after receiving a verbal lashing from his boss. He displaces his feelings by kicking open the front door, spanking his children because they are being too noisy, and creating an argument with his wife over a trivial and unimportant matter such as the fact that the bathroom sink could use a cleaning.

Throughout history, humankind has been led by unscrupulous individuals who have acted on this weak trait of taking frustrations and insecurities out on others. Finding a scapegoat upon which to place the sins of a people has been a popular "sport" since ancient times; and unfortunately, it still exists. Whenever you see unwarranted emotions displayed in a negotiation, they may well be the result of displacement.

## Repression

The exclusion from conscious thought of feelings and wishes that are repugnant or painful to the individual is called repression. This process is not intentional; it is unconscious. The convenient "forgetting" of an unpleasant past event or future duty is an example. Sigmund Freud, the father of psychoanalysis, insisted that forgetting is motivated and not accidental.

Certainly repression is at work when a person suddenly remembers an appointment that was bound to be disagreeable, but she conveniently only remembers it after the time for keeping it has passed. A good negotiator, of course, would know quite well that the other party did not want to attend. While repression is generally unintentional, it can be very damaging to a professional situation.

# Reaction Formation

Reaction formation is a possible follow-up to repression. People often repress strong, unacceptable drives, then think and act in ways that are in precise opposition to these repressed drives. The latter is termed reaction formation because the individual forms her behavior in reaction to something she is trying to mask. Again, bear in mind that the repression is entirely unconscious, and thus so is the reaction formation.

In *Hamlet,* we have a famous example of reaction formation. Queen Gertrude, Hamlet's mother, who is a very sexual creature, bombastically protests that she will never marry again if her husband should die. Meanwhile, she is not truly in love with the man, as is later evidenced by her marriage to the king's brother very shortly after the king's death. So her speech does not truthfully reflect her heart. Here, we can apply the often-quoted comment, "The lady doth protest too much, methinks." Negotiators sometimes see this type of exaggerated behavior at the negotiating table. For example, a party might try so hard not to appear greedy or aggressive that she behaves in a saccharine, patronizing, or even dishonest manner.

# Role Playing

In this context, role-playing is a little different than what you might do in a theatre class. In terms of basic human behavior, role-playing involves acting out a role based mostly on previous experiences an individual has had in her life. The individual has a preconceived notion of how she should act or react in a given situation, and she fulfills that expectation. For example, a man who is called upon to act the role of a father and administer punishment to his young son will usually act the way his own father did; he applies what he knows as "fatherly behavior" based on his experience.

Of course, sometimes a man might act in exactly the opposite way his father did, which would tend to be a type of reaction formation, discussed above. It largely depends on what the individual's childhood conception of punishment was—how fair it seemed, how gentle or abusive it was perceived to be, how it matched with her own personality traits and tendencies. Often there is a faint conception of what role the individual wants to play but is not quite accomplishing because of influence either from the past or from others. Usually, when in doubt that we're satisfying our own expectations, we seem to work out a role that satisfies us by using the trial and error method.

A negotiator has to be keenly aware of role-playing behavior. Someone might irrationally fly into a rage, but only as part of a routine that person learned from past experiences. Perhaps in previous negotiations such behavior was effective because it made the other side nervous and ultimately more amenable to change. It will take a lot of patience and emotional control for the negotiator on the receiving end not to react in a like manner. Knowing that the rage could simply be part of a learned behavioral pattern might give that second negotiator the courage to lead the enraged party away from such behavior by not playing into its expectations.

Certainly, the behaviors described in this section are not behaviors specifically attributed to the negotiation process. However, learning about them can help us understand people more thoroughly and read people more effectively. Then, we ultimately can conduct negotiations more quickly and satisfyingly. But don't think the behaviors explored above are all we need to worry about. As if these behaviors didn't make things complicated enough, some psychologists have advised that when two people interact, there are actually six different personalities involved. According to such behavioral experts, it's because each person has three different personalities: (1) the person she is; (2) the person she thinks she is (self-image); (3) and the person she appears to be. No wonder it can be so difficult to negotiate with another human being!

As negotiators, this knowledge is valuable to us because, at a bargaining session, we can look for the three-fold personality aspects in each person. Once we become sensitive to the complexity of human behavior and the fact that we are dealing with a multiplicity of personalities in each individual, negotiations become much easier to manage. We see others with a stronger set of reading glasses, so to speak.

## REDEFINING "RATIONAL BEHAVIOR"

When it comes to assessing individuals, quirky behavior is one thing, but "crazy" behavior is another. Yet in truth, a lot of what we write off as irrational might just be unfamiliar to us. So we challenge you not to automatically label unfamiliar behavior as irrational. Behavior should not be labeled as irrational until you have explored the assumptions and premises upon which you are basing that call. You might simply be dealing with cultural differences or witnessing a true misunderstanding. We will give you an extreme example of cultural differences to illustrate this point.

At the start of most negotiations, individuals usually shake hands. If they know each other very well, they may even hug. Such conduct openly signals a cordial greeting and is considered rational behavior. However, if you were ever to negotiate in a home or small dwelling anywhere in Tibet other than a major city, you would be greeted by a person who would stick her tongue out at you. What would your initial reaction be?

To an American, such behavior would be very irrational; it does not conform to an American's assumptions and expectations. Since childhood, we assign a particular nonverbal meaning to this gesture. Sticking out the tongue is used to taunt, offend, or mock someone. But there is an age-old superstition in Tibet concerning individuals who poison their guests. The belief is that such individuals have dark tongues. Therefore, when greeting guests, a Tibetan host will stick out her tongue to show that it is not dark and visitors need not fear being poisoned. Knowing that, what looked like irrational behavior now becomes quite acceptable.

Louis D. Brandeis must have experienced this in his worldly travels, because he once stated, "Nine-tenths of the serious controversies which arise in life result from misunderstanding. They result from a person not knowing the facts which to the other person seem important; they also fail to appreciate the other person's point of view."

Whether we like it or not, we humans tend to behave in accordance with our individual version of rationality. As a result of this, we are likely to refer to a person as "irrational" if, in our opinion, she acts in ways and with options that are not available to us as "normal." Our judgment is fundamentally based on whether or not we know and understand the premises and standards by which the person behaves. Consider the following stories that present situations and people many of us would initially judge as irrational.

# A Cracked-Up Coach

Several years ago we read of a high school football coach who did something "irrational" and turned the team's looming defeat into a win. He motivated his team by his unusual behavior. The team was undefeated and had won ten consecutive games; the local newspapers had hailed the players as "the team of the decade." It was the final game of the season, and they were playing a team who had lost eight out of ten games played. The undefeated team was a favorite to win by a more than thirty points. Yet, it was half time and they were behind by a score of twenty to three.

The discouraged and dejected team was settled in the dressing room and expecting a verbal tongue-lashing from their highly spirited coach. Therefore, they were completely shocked when he exhibited quite comedic behavior. He was smiling, dancing around, and singing, "They're going to beat your ass and I know why." After several choruses of the same words he stopped and asked the team a question. "Do you know why they're beating your ass so badly?" One player had the courage to ask, and the coach responded, "Those stupid players don't know how to read. Therefore, they don't know who the hell you are! They're not aware you are considered the greatest high school team this state has ever had. And because of this, they're going to whip your ass soundly!"

The coach's "irrational" behavior actually delivered a poignant message. His point came through loud and clear. And his team won the game, remaining undefeated for the entire season.

# An Insightful Inmate

Jerry has often told the story of a man whose automobile tire went flat outside a healthcare facility for the insane. As the driver got out of his car to change the tire, one of the inmates stood inside the property's fence and watched him. The driver removed the wheel lugs and carefully placed each one of them in the hubcap, which was lying on the traffic side of the road. As he went to get the spare tire, a car sped by and hit the hubcap, scattering the wheel lugs in all directions.

After several minutes of looking, the man who drove the car was still unable to find the wheel lugs. He was bewildered and scratched his head, wondering what to do next. The facility's patient, who had been watching everything that had occurred, yelled, "Hey mister, take one lug off the other wheels and put them on the spare tire. I may be crazy, but I'm not stupid!"

Now how many of us would assume that a resident of an insane asylum could solve a practical problem for us? Unfortunately, most would assume that he wouldn't have much to contribute along the lines of practical, wise advice. Yet this story teaches us not to make too many quick assumptions. You never know the extent of a stranger's problem-solving capacity, so it might be worth your while to give every person a fair shot.

What or who we might first judge as irrational could be very rational, calculated, or intelligent indeed. This section on redefining what's rational challenges us to open our eyes and see behaviors and people in a new light. That way we can withhold harmful judgments during negotiations and be more responsible negotiators.

## BREAKING DOWN BARRIERS

Failing to understand people's premises and judging them or their behaviors as irrational is certainly one challenge to overcome when you are learning to be a successful negotiator. Humans like boxes—we think they are neat and handy—so we tend to put others in boxes and label them. Then there are the boxes or barriers we tend to place around ourselves. And that presents a whole new set of challenges.

Ask a group of kindergarten children if they can paint or sing, and notice that the majority will raise their hands in expressing that they can. Then take a classroom of adults attending night school and ask them the same question. You'll see very few raised hands. That clearly illustrates the barriers adults build around themselves.

We tend to believe in the imaginary lines we place around others and ourselves too readily and for too long. The following story illustrates this. A farmer put up an electrified fence around his pasture. A year later, his neighbor complimented him on the fence because cows tended not to go near it—the farmer's cows were staying right where he wanted them to stay. The neighbor also explained that while the fence was very efficient, it would not be practical for his own farm because he could not afford the electrical expense such a fence incurred. The farmer laughed at his neighbor and said, "Don't let that bother you. I turned off the electricity the second day, and those cows never knew it!"

We can be like those cows, and so can the people with whom we negotiate. Humans are creatures of habit and, furthermore, creatures of fear who often don't push the envelope or take a risk. To negotiate successfully, we need to conduct the process with as few barriers as possible. We need to have a "can-do" attitude. Such a frame of mind sets the stage for creativity that is sorely needed and required in order to overcome the many obstacles we have to encounter and deal with in a professional and capable manner.

Many books have been written on the nature and application of creativity— its origin, formulation, environment, plus many other factors—without nailing down a fundamental formula of how to acquire it. Creativity is really too creative to fully define! However, there are several types of environments that can safely be blamed for draining and/or preventing creativity. These include environments that are highly stressful or full of tension; environments that are too familiar, and therefore don't encourage us to try new things; and environments that induce fear, whether due to aggressive personalities or uncomfortable surroundings. The reason a person will often close her eyes in a dark room is simply because she is more comfortable not seeing than witnessing the strangeness that exists with her eyes wide open. Again, the barriers are more comfortable.

In negotiations, be wary of the person who states, "This is the only (or best) way of doing this!" It is a clear sign of someone who intellectually is closing the door to any options or alternatives. Many years ago the individual who was the head of the U.S. Patent Office retired. When he was asked why he was leaving, he foolishly answered, "Because everything that is worthwhile has been invented!" Closing the mind to possibility also closes the mind to creativity. Therefore, it is important to chip away at the basic human tendency to erect and maintain boundaries that keep us attached to old ways of doing and seeing things.

## STUDYING MOTIVATION

So far, this chapter has emphasized the complexity of human behavior—how varied and multileveled it is. But now we turn to something quite straightforward and something that everyone shares: motivation. People are motivated by different things, but as discussed earlier, we all have needs and therefore are all motivated to satisfy those needs. In fact, needs are the fundamental source of motivation in all negotiations and in life. Let's study several factors that affect motivation, including emotions, the desire for power, and the quest to enhance our own self-esteem, and the thrill of a challenge.

## The Role of Emotions

The one common ingredient among the various needs discussed in this chapter is an emotional source and influence. *Feelings* often take precedence over *thinking*. There is no stronger element in motivation and negotiations than emotions.

For example, the person you have been bargaining with for several days all of a sudden threatens to back out of the deal. Or the dealer who has just sold you a new car explains certain things are not covered by the warranty. What do you do in either case? Get angry and start shouting? Your emotions have just been triggered.

How you respond is very important. At such times, the motivation to make a deal can easily be extinguished by a few spoken words.

There are many psychologists who have truthfully stated how difficult it is to actually define emotions. People think that they know what emotions are, but when asked for a definition, they realize they don't really know! Furthermore, most people don't often think about how ambiguous our emotional capacity is; our emotions are so complex that they can create both positive and negative effects in the same moment. They can make us feel great, and they can make us feel like we're in the pits, and very quickly at that.

When negotiating, we not only have to worry about our own emotions but also the emotions of everyone else in the room. Positive emotions motivate us to cooperate and become friendly with the other party. If we exude positive emotions, we are likely to put the other side at ease and in a more generous spirit. Displaying negative emotions causes us to appear argumentative and unfriendly. Such emotions can be obstacles in our negotiations. The great difficulty is that all of us have negative emotions. We simply must learn to manage them. Emotions are capable of turning a negotiation "on a dime," from heading toward a settlement to careening toward a possible walkout.

When a person becomes visibly and audibly angry—or even upset—everyone's interest in and attention to matters change. As negotiators, we must be prepared to deal with the other party's emotional outbursts if such a situation unfortunately arises. We have to react in a positive and discreet manner, which is not easy in such a situation. Should you apologize? Tell them off? Smile at them and perhaps make them angrier?

We negotiated once with a lady who handled such a situation in a very creative and expert manner—she used humor. A man from an opposing party in the negotiation became very angry, stood up, and glared at everyone on the other side of the table. His face turned as red as a beet and, while staring at her, he shouted, "You're trying to screw me!" She smiled at him and said, "I thought it was supposed to be the other way around!" Everyone involved in the negotiation laughed, including the angry man, who promptly sat down. The negotiation continued.

Again, whenever positive emotions are used in a negotiation, the parties involved are naturally motivated to be more cooperative and compromising. An atmosphere of shared needs is created, which replaces an attitude of "me" and "mine." Positive emotions also create an environment in which people are more open to listening, instead of simply talking. And, usually, when individuals listen well, they are more receptive to ideas and thoughts that serve common needs instead of individual interests.

## The Thirst for Power

We have met many negotiators during the course of our careers, and those who stand out in our minds are the ones who were not motivated by the acquisition of power or money. Instead, they were highly motivated to achieve compromises and settlements through expert persuasion. They were truly good at reading people and bringing contentment to all sides.

The word *power* has different meanings. However, the one most usually associated with it is control and dominance over others. Seldom will you ever find someone who uses the word *persuasion* in her definition of power. Yet that's the perspective we negotiators need to take ourselves and encourage in others. Famous television writer and producer Norman Lear once said during an interview, "Power is the ability to persuade, and if one fails at persuading, that person is not thrown out with the effort. It seems to me there can be no greater power than in persuasion; to communicate . . . to reach them."

Whenever achieving power is the motivating factor in a person's life, it is indeed a very complex matter. Power may mean being "top dog" in an organization. Or it might mean being the voice and mind behind the "top dog." The questions we must ask ourselves are, "But is the finish line of a race to the top all that matters? Is outperforming others and/or running over them actually an act of healthy, effective power?"

Power, to some, means being important, being noticed, or being taken seriously. It may also mean the ability to give orders and have others carry them out. But to most successful negotiators, power exists in the achievement and self-worth that comes from conducting a negotiation in which everybody wins something, when everyone walks away satisfied yet knowing some "little bit" was left on the table. One of our favorite expressions of power was stated by renowned publisher Malcolm Forbes:

> Leadership involves power. You're not the leader if you don't have the power; if you don't have the decision-making authority. People who like authority for itself are never successful, but exercising authority is part of what is required from somebody in a responsible position. You've got to be able to do it, but when it's an end in itself, usually you're not successful.

## The Desire to Enhance Self-Image

Self-image is certainly involved in feeling and being powerful. It is also inherently involved in motivation. Esteem is one of Maslow's basic needs, mentioned earlier in this chapter. And self-esteem is a big part of that need. The human need to feel good about one's self-image is a great motivator. It is healthy to need to view oneself as being significant, different from others, someone who can stand out and make things happen. It is a person's self-image that motivates her to take risks and face challenges; she desires a strong feeling of self-worth and capability.

Many years ago, when General Electric looked to see what motivated their research staff, they discovered that "recognition" was at the top of the list. A person who had done a good piece of work wants to have it recognized. Status and recognition—often associated with positions of power—are known to be powerful motivators because they are rewards that nourish the self-image. But it's important to realize that status is not the same as power. Status is more about simple acknowledgement, while power is something much more profound.

## The Thrill of a Challenge

Often, when we do something worthwhile and outstanding, we receive recognition for the accomplishment. That recognition often comes in the form of praise from co-workers and/or other peer groups. However, we have to recognize that there is difference between having a drive for success and being driven by it. Most of us can recall someone who was highly motivated (driven) to get revenge. Whenever that is the source, achieving the goal is not nearly as sweet as when it is achieved because of an inner drive for success.

And that inner drive seems to work much better when we establish or visualize a target. The reason for this is very simple: a target is the acceptance of a challenge. For example, an athlete competing in the Olympic Games establishes an inner target of winning a gold medal and visualizes it. Instead of mentally drifting around, there is something definite to be done; there is almost something therapeutic about the concentration that is required and the creativity used to reach a settlement. There is a target to shoot at that represents a measure to gauge our achievement and success.

For some of us, sharp focus on a specific negotiation is something we desire. An outstanding negotiator we know mentioned to us that before each negotiation, she visualizes concluding the meeting by seeing smiles on the faces of the other persons involved. She firmly believes that if that inner picture becomes a reality, she will have fulfilled every objective she had in mind and the results will be successful.

Yes, a negotiation provides an opportunity to reduce our complex world to a specific challenge and to overcome it. Accepting the challenge thus becomes a motivating factor. For the most part, humans are goal-driven, and a challenge triggers a "can-do" mental attitude in a healthy individual.

There are strong links between basic needs, emotions, power, self-image, and an invigorating challenge when it comes to motivation. And all of those aspects influence each other. One thing we really want you to retain from this discussion on motivation is the importance of postivity. There have been times when we commenced a negotiation with both sides voicing their respective beliefs, feelings, and motives in a very positive manner. And the attitude served as a firm foundation for a negotiation that ultimately concluded with everyone winning and being satisfied. Positivity breeds greater motivation.

By the way, we have also been witness to some negotiations that started out with a very powerful negative attitude, which we later discovered was simply an opening tactic. The "opening salvo" was something like this: "We firmly believe that not much will result by sitting down with you and negotiating this mess—a mess you guys have put us in. It is against our better judgment to . . . !" We'll let you fill in the words. Whatever motivation such individuals had behind their drive to negotiate was not very positive. It was important for us not to let such negative motivation take away from our own sense of power and success, from our own positive emotions, and from our own healthy self-images. We had to keep in mind that everyone has needs that motivate them, but we don't all have to seek to answer those needs in the same way.

Motivation is the source of inner energy that drives a person to accomplish something. Of course, persistence is what ultimately assists her in overcoming obstacles and succeeding. As the old expression says, "If at first you don't succeed, try, try again." There is a great deal of truth in that worn out message.

## CONCLUSION

If we want to understand people more fully, it is essential to deal with elements that are common to all of us, namely basic human needs and how to satisfy those needs. These are the keys to the art of negotiating. Hopefully, this chapter has allowed you to learn about both, to become better at reading others, to focus more fully on positivity, and to be motivated to be successful according to the big picture, not in pursuit of wealth and fame. Now we're ready to narrow our general study of human behavior and look at negotiators in particular. What makes a person a successful negotiator?

# 3

# The Profile of a Successful Negotiator
## Talents and Traits

*"To be successful, you have to be able to relate to people;*
*they have to be satisfied with your personality to*
*be able to do business with you and to build*
*a relationship with mutual trust."*

—GEORGE ROSS

O ver the years that we have been negotiating and giving seminars on the topic of negotiating, we have met all sorts of people. They have been of all skill levels and talents. And watching them, we have been able to observe what works and what doesn't. With that information, we have developed a profile of the successful negotiator. In this chapter, we'll share that profile with you so that you can aim toward being the most successful negotiator you can be.

There are numerous talents and personality traits that are involved in such a profile. It would be foolish to rank the importance of the various aspects because they are all important at one time or another during the course of a negotiation. So this chapter does not organize the elements of the profile in any ascending or descending order. Instead, we start by pointing out particular communication talents that we consistently find in people who are master negotiators. Then we offer you a comprehensive collection of personality characteristics that are typical of the successful negotiator.

## IDENTIFYING KEY TALENTS

Successful negotiators come in many different shapes, sizes, and styles. They come from many different backgrounds and serve many different purposes. However, there are certain talents that successful negotiators seem to share. Many of these talents have to do with the art of communicating—asking effective questions, listening attentively, gathering information wisely. Others have to do with artful speech and leadership skills.

While some people are born with these talents, others must work hard at developing them. The important part is that you *can* hone such skills, so you should never just accept the fact that you aren't particularly gifted in any of these areas. This section serves as a valuable guide concerning what to work on if you are on the track to becoming an expert negotiator.

## The Right Questions

As we have already emphasized, needs are what fuel every negotiation, whether that negotiation is between individuals, small companies, large organizations, or nations. When a negotiation begins, everyone fundamentally understands that both surface-level and deeply rooted needs will cause whatever conflict or compromises result. They also are aware that once needs are satisfied, settlements and agreements usually follow. The hard work is finding the best way to reach satisfaction for all parties.

During our seminars, we mention that one of the most important things a person must discover during the course of a negotiation is the other party's needs, as opposed to their wants. Wording is very important at a time when the differences are small and a negotiator can "smell a settlement." As mentioned previously in this book, an effective negotiator should ask, "Now that you have told us what you want, what do you really need?" It is absolutely amazing how, once faced with such a direct question, individuals clearly understand the difference between those words. And as a result of this awareness, those individuals will almost always lower their demands (wants) and settle for their actual needs, which are less. Have you ever met someone whose wants were not greater than his needs?

The successful negotiator knows how to get into someone's head; he develops an intuitive idea of what that person is thinking. Jerry has often recommended an excellent book titled *Getting Through to People,* written by Jesse S. Nierenberg (no relation). It gives valuable information on the skill of picking up clues and tip-offs during a negotiation. Certainly, an expert negotiator is a mental detective, and part of being a good detective is possessing good questioning skills. Asking poignant questions is just as important as discreetly gathering clues.

Moreover, the successful negotiator is skilled in asking questions not only for purposes of recognizing needs but also to obtain other information that is required. In our research on negotiations, we have found that the best questions pass the "what, how, and when" test that should be conducted before the actual negotiation, during the preparation phase. The "what" discusses precisely which question to ask and the individual who will ask it. The "how" covers weighing the words of the question carefully. Finally, the "when" refers to the timing of the question, which is so important.

For example, if you were to ask the question that reveals the difference between a party's wants and needs too early in a negotiation, it probably would get you nothing. However, if you asked it after several hours of haggling, at a time when both sides are edging towards an agreement, it is likely to be far more effective. A negotiator does not need to qualify as a professional interrogator. However, he does need to understand the five categories into which questions fall:

1. **General questions:** "What do you think?" "Why did you do that?" Such questions pose no limits, and the person who asks them cannot control the answers at all.

2. **Direct questions:** "Who is responsible?" "Who will handle the assignment?" A very effective one is, "What do you recommend?" These questions usually get direct responses.

3. **Leading questions:** "Don't you agree that . . . ?" "Isn't it a fact that . . . ?" These questions put the inquirer in somewhat of a power position because he is setting the responder up in a particular direction.

4. **Fact-finding questions:** "Where?" "Who?" "When?" "What?" "How?" "Why?" These questions allow you to gather all the basic data you need. The first three cannot be controlled by the asker, but the last two can sometimes be guided.

5. **Opinion-seeking questions:** "In your opinion . . . ?" "What do you think of . . . ?" "What would you like to see happen?" These questions allow you to probe the other side for information on what would fulfill their direst needs and their most impractical wants.

The use of questions is a powerful and useful negotiating tool and must be used accordingly—with discretion and judgment. The improper use of this tool will always create problems and lead to difficult circumstances. Over the course of his many years of experience as a lawyer, Jerry learned to stay away from uncontrollable questions during a cross-examination—that is, questions that disallowed him any control in guiding the answer. Instead, he would ask questions that generated straightforward information and disclosure. Certainly, disclosure plays an extremely important part in every negotiation.

The manner in which a question is asked will lead to the type and amount of information received. Learning to control the tone of questions is similar to turning a water faucet on and controlling the flow of water. This is simply because questions stimulate others to think within a certain context or mood. And if that context or mood is positive, you just might hit the jackpot!

In addition, if you are conducting a team-type negotiation that involves superior and subordinate organizational members, it is very important to discuss who will ask which questions. During this part of the preparation, it is also wise to remember that questions have a tendency to trigger emotional responses. So when you prepare your questions, try to anticipate which ones will elicit strong responses that might require a little appeasement or distraction in order to get through the wake of the storm.

We cannot emphasize enough that there are times when questions create problems because they touch sensitive nerves, causing emotional and hostile reactions. Jerry learned this when he asked a lady what he considered to be a simple question: "When were you born?" At the time, he and the woman were both in the act of completing a questionnaire. She reacted in a very violent manner, apparently offended that he would even think to ask. For just a moment, Jerry thought the woman might actually hit him with any object she could grab.

Jerry's experience taught him a valuable lesson. In some instances, whenever a question is about to be asked, it would be worthwhile thinking twice about how to ask it. Perhaps you should preface the question with information on why you are asking it in the first place. For example, you could use such statements as, "In order to better understand why you feel that way, I need to know . . .", or "Perhaps I can understand your situation better if you tell me. . . ." If these introductory statements are used before the actual question is asked, you will become much more successful when presenting sensitive inquiries.

Indeed, it is good practice to explain the reason for asking a question. It avoids trouble and possible embarrassment to you and/or the other person. Of course, it is possible to avoid a plethora of unpleasant responses to your questions if you avoid accusatory and arrogant wording such as, "What is your excuse?" and "What do you have to say for yourself now?"

One of the questions Hank most hated to hear when growing up was, "Have you learned your lesson yet?" It seemed so condescending, and he unfortunately heard it on many occasions. One day when an older brother used it, Hank answered, "No, because I haven't finished school yet!" Then Hank simply walked away. By the way, he never had an adult member of his family ever ask that question again.

Well-conceived and concise questions are powerful tools for prying information out of individuals. They often lead others to reveal motives and hidden needs that will be very important along the road to reaching an agreement or settlement. But another caution is necessary: be extremely prudent when asking questions that sound like they contain implications, even vaguely. Your tone of voice and your choice of words have to be carefully considered, especially in a very sensitive situation. Otherwise, your questions might work to your great disadvantage.

And finally, those impromptu questions which are "shot from the hip" during the course of a negotiation may result in "shooting yourself in the foot!" You cannot overestimate the importance of preparation when it comes to developing and asking questions. The skillful use of questions can save you from hidden assumptions you made that could have undermined your needs and objectives. But the poor use of questions can put the other side on the defensive and leave you in a more vulnerable position than when you started. The successful negotiator knows the power of asking the right questions, in the right way.

## Effective Listening

Listening is the flipside in the communication process. And Mother Nature has clearly told us which side is of greater importance, for as the saying goes, "That's why she gave us two ears and one mouth." The successful negotiator knows that listening is a key part of the negotiation process. By listening effectively, a negotiator can pick up on subtle needs and wants, convince the opposing party of his interest and fairness, and judge how aggressive and how compromising to be.

We have researched a great amount of written material on the subject of listening skills. All of it was worthwhile reading. However, none of the books we have studied ever mentions the subject of "silent talking." So what is it? It's what so many of us are doing when we think we're listening. Unconsciously, we are mentally speaking while appearing to be listening.

During our seminars, whenever we cover the subject of listening, we emphasize that silent talking is counterproductive in any situation in which an individual must hear and clearly understand the entire message being communicated. And we suggest a technique that can help you to minimize silent talking whenever you wish. Try the following scenario.

Imagine that you have never jumped out of an airplane, much less packaged a parachute for possible use. You are attending a class in which the instructor will not only tell you how to package a parachute but also how to properly use it when you jump. There will be no questions asked and you must listen carefully and understand each step in order to survive, because it is almost certain you will soon have to jump from an aircraft.

After this scenario is given at our seminars, we ask; "How many of you think you would listen extremely well and not miss a single thing said?" As you probably guessed, everyone raises his hand. Then we explain, "Now, the next time you are having a very serious conversation that requires extreme attention in order not to miss a single word that is said, simply remember the parachute example. Make believe it is an equally serious matter that requires your undivided attention. Doing so will help you to silence the mental talking that distracts the mind and prevents you from being the best listener you can be."

Another aspect of listening that is important is realizing that, whenever people speak, there are nuances in their messages. Nuances are subtleties; they are indirect but important distinctions we tuck into our phrasing. During a negotiation, what individuals say may have various levels of meaning, much like the way a dream might have various levels of meaning. The famed psychoanalyst Sigmund Freud postulated that a dream can be interpreted on three different levels. Similarly, when speaking, a person's statement can be multidimensional. As an example, if someone states: "We might be open to a proposal," there's the up-front level of meaning that is exactly what we hear. But on the second level, that person is stating that he is indeed willing to consider offers. And finally, on the third level, he's saying, "Let's negotiate."

During the last few decades, many institutions have been offering courses in listening skills. In those classes, participants discuss three very interesting conclusions that negotiators should be aware of: (1) we are able to listen four times faster than we can talk; (2) we retain only a relatively small percentage of what we hear; (3) when listening, concentration is very brief—less than thirty seconds. We agree that listening is a difficult process—even during a negotiation, when we need to hang onto every word. It's too bad those classes haven't also included the subject of negotiating in their curriculum.

The negotiator who learns how to listen well will benefit greatly from it. We would like to pass along to you what information we have gathered from thousands of seminar attendees on ways and means of becoming better listeners. First, quite a few attendees have advised, "Listen with a critical mind that is open to suggestions." That means you should mentally separate facts, premises, assumptions, and perceptions into specific categories without saying a single word. It is somewhat like being a chess player, seeing a move made in a game and thinking not only about the move but about everything behind why it was made, as well as what the next move might be. By actively listening and working to place all the content into categories, you will be gaining crucial information and constantly adjusting your tactics. The mental ping-pong balls will be in constant motion. And by remaining open to suggestions, you don't automatically eliminate some of what you hear.

Second, do not stop listening to ideas simply because you don't like them. Instead, give them a second thought. If you still don't like them, give them one more chance. In a sincere and honest manner say, "On the surface, I don't like the idea, but before I completely reject it, tell me more." This suggestion may be worthwhile not only to practice during negotiations but also in personal relationships.

And the third suggestion we hear quite often is in regard to a team-type negotiation. When a negotiator is part of a team, he not only has to listen to the opposing party but also to what another person on his own side is saying. He must listen for the purpose of making sure his teammate is pursuing the same negotiating strategy as previously planned. When a teammate is veering away from the set plan, it is important to interrupt him in order to get back on course, but to do so as subtly and quickly as possible. The key here is "listening ahead." This means that you are listening with the intent of understanding what your teammate is saying *and* where he is headed.

We have our very own suggestions as well. Indeed, questions that tend to cement relationships are very important because they not only bring individuals together but they also clear the air of any misunderstandings that may exist. Whenever we ask questions or make requests such as, "We have discussed many issues and other matters today. Which ones are the most important to you?", or "I would greatly appreciate it if you explained . . . ", we are developing fertile ground for possible settlements. We are also showing that we want to listen deeply to the needs and wants of the other side. That fosters trust and, ultimately, successful negotiations. Offering to listen deeply to the other party is a stark contrast to the type of questions used when a negotiator puts the other person on the hot seat or the witness chair and creates greater hostility and defensiveness.

And the last suggestion involving listening that we offer you is always to listen for *meta-talk* throughout your negotiations. We co-authored a book called *MetaTalk*. The term refers to the hidden agenda in a conversation, and there are many in every negotiation. Meta-talk is so common that it can be heard daily, everywhere in our society. We frequently hear expressions like, "By the way . . . " or "Before I forget . . . " when the speaker wants us to believe that what he is about to say just entered his mind and isn't of great importance to him. In reality, it *is* of significant importance. That's meta-talk. And when someone begins a sentence with such words as, "To be honest . . . ," "To tell the truth . . . ," or "Frankly . . . ," chances are that person is *not* being frank or honest.

People often use meta-talk as a means of covering up something. When listening, we must be sensitive enough to sense the speaker's subconscious meaning and motivation when he uses such meta-talk expressions. What we both don't understand is why the expression "Don't give me that meta-talk!" has not become a phrase commonly used!

To sum up this section on the importance of listening in all of our relationships, we will use a wonderful quote from respected American psychologist Carl Rogers: "If I can listen to what he tells me, if I can understand how it seems to him, if I can sense the emotional flavor which it has for him, then I will be releasing potent forces of change within him." An expert negotiator knows the power of listening. He uses it to enhance his knowledge, his persuasiveness, and his reputation.

## Effective Speech

Now it's time to discuss what happens when we "vibrate air molecules"—that is, when we speak. There are more positive metaphors for speech than the one we just offered, and we should mention one for balance. Unfortunately, we don't remember who described speech in the following way, but it is quite beautiful: "Speak so that I may see your mind in parade." Actually, effective speech is a beautiful and wonderful thing. However, it's also very difficult, because what we say is multilayered.

First, there is our actual word choice and the statements that come out of our mouths. Then there is what we meant to say, what we implied, and the like. Finally, there is what the other person hears and what he believes we meant. In many instances there is a disparity somewhere between the three—the layers don't stack up correctly.

Communication, if anything, is a social thing. The spread of information through a group of people is one of the most important events that can occur. Because of this, the psychology of communication should be taught in schools and universities. And such a course should begin with the reasons why communication is so important, not only when professionally negotiating but also in all interpersonal relationships. The course should emphasize that our words are very powerful because they greatly influence and affect the actions, behavior, and thoughts of others. When things go wrong, it may be because the speaker was responsible for "lighting the fuse"—or using the words—that set off the explosion.

Indeed, one simple word may have a myriad of meanings. As an example, consider the word *Dutch*. Ever since the seventh-century naval rivalry between the Dutch and English, the English have used the word Dutch as an epithet of derision. When used today, it may mean "in trouble," as in a Dutch widow—a prostitute; a Dutch bargain—a deal made when drunk; Dutch courage—bravery produced by alcohol; a Dutch treat— when each person pays for himself; and Dutch comfort—which means no comfort at all.

An interesting theory about the origin of language in the human race proposes that speech imitates gestures normally made with the arms and head. Suppose, for instance, a primitive human wanted to make a beckoning gesture but it was dark, or his hands were full, or his companion was not looking at him. In such a situation, the primitive human would then make a vocal noise and "vibrate air molecules." We probably will never know whether this theory is correct or not, but it sure sounds logical.

The one thing we do know is that words are signs that conveniently represent the objects or ideas people have in mind. In short, listeners respond to spoken words in the same way they respond to other stimuli that impinge on their receptor organs, whether that is heat, cold, noise, or something else. And what makes verbal communication more difficult is that words have an arbitrary significance; they can only signify to us what we have learned. There has to be a context for the words.

At a particular negotiation, an intelligent and learned individual was verbally attacked when someone yelled to him, "Don't give me all that damn gibberish!" There was a moment of silence, as no one knew what to say. Then the erudite negotiator responded very softly, "Sir, the word *gibberish* is a corruption of the word *jabber*. It was once referred to as 'the mystic language of Geber; a reference to Jabir ibn Hayyan, an eighth-century chemist who is reputed to have written more than 2,000 books. The likely explanation for the word is to give authority to his works. I consider your comment a compliment!" You could have heard a pin drop in the silence that followed. In a short time, the negotiation was successfully concluded, and the person who used the word *gibberish* said little else.

The moral of the story is that you might not please everyone with your words or your approaches. However, if you are concise, clear, and intelligent in your presentation, there's not much they can say against you. Choose your words wisely, as words are complex and dynamic—that is, multilayered and, to a certain degree, individually interpreted.

Effective speech, or good communication, in a negotiation is especially important because it establishes credibility. The seeds of trust are nurtured by the words we use during the process of explaining, demanding, answering, questioning, plus much more during the course of a negotiation. An individual's tendency to accept what you have told him will depend in part on how he feels towards you regarding your knowledge, credibility, expertise, trustworthiness and experience—all of which may be quickly destroyed by whatever you say. That's how important it is for a negotiator to communicate clearly and concisely. And the interesting result we have observed is that when negotiators have achieved a high self-esteem level as effective communicators, they appear to be natural at effective speech. Aldous Huxley described this very well when he wrote, "Words are magical in the way they affect the mind of those who use them."

## Insightful Fact-Finding

Most successful negotiators excel in their efforts to acquire information about the individuals and organizations with whom they will negotiate. Obviously, knowing a great deal about the other side, especially their needs, is a huge asset. The area in which most of us can improve is in gathering more information about the specific individual(s) involved. When the negotiation will involve only one other person, it is much easier than when the negotiator has to deal with multiple people, their personalities, styles of communication, and particular needs.

Another reason for difficulties in gathering information on the other party and its perspective is something that books, courses, and lectures on communication don't cover: *abstracting*. This is a process in which we select some details while completely disregarding others. Abstracting not only occurs in listening, but also in reading and seeing. Each of us has abstracting tendencies when hearing, looking, and even touching.

A perfect example of this found in "The Blind Men and the Elephant" by John Godfrey Saxe. The story is about six blind individuals who were asked to touch an elephant and then describe what they believed it was. The first touched its side and said it was a wall. The second touched a tusk and proclaimed the elephant to be a spear. The third touched the squirming trunk and exclaimed, "It's a snake!" The fourth felt a leg and pronounced that it felt like a tree. The fifth one touched an ear and responded, "It feels like a fan!" And the last one touched the tail and reported that the object was very much like a rope.

The individuals who have the most difficult task in dealing with abstracting are the police, when they must question individuals who are at the scene of a crime. Trying to arrive at a picture of what specifically occurred at the crime scene—regarding who, what and when—is made considerably more difficult because each person has abstracted different information. In negotiations, abstracting while listening often leads to making incorrect assumptions, a subject covered later in the book.

Whenever we become familiar with something we tend to be less observant. That's the principle reason for abstracting. And that is why a visitor to where you live may notice something in your neighborhood that you have never seen, despite the fact that you have lived there for many years. Alfred Korzybski, a great writer, mathematician, and scientist, gave us some wonderful advice when he wrote, "Treat the familiar as unfamiliar." Hank follows his advice each morning during his walk and discovers something he had not noticed before, such as the strange shape of a tree or a new person walking on the usual path.

How does this apply to negotiating? Even negotiators tend to get into their own habits and grooves. There's so much to think about regarding the legal and financial aspects of a negotiation that we tend to put the "human" aspect last. In fact, we might not even bother to do extra research on the individuals involved in a negotiation. Yet finding out facts about the people representing and arguing for each party is an invaluable tactic. Most negotiators go into a negotiation aware of the other side's activities, market, products, operation, and other aspects of their business, yet sadly lacking on the individuals—their personality traits, habits, and professional backgrounds.

A seminar attendee once told us a great story about this matter. She had been negotiating for several days with a chief executive on an agreement to license the company's product. Her firm had marketing outlets in certain foreign markets and was very successful.

However, there were three other firms also competing to acquire the license. So she had to figure out a way to go the extra mile and grab the executive's attention. In her fact-finding research she discovered the executive's son was attending the same university from which she graduated. During their first in-person meeting, they spoke about their common connection to that university before they covered more serious matters. Our negotiator subsequently had two other meetings with the executive, as did her competitors.

A month later, the executive called the woman into his office to tell her that her firm would receive the foreign licensing for his company's products. She knew before the first meeting that there were larger firms she was competing with and that her chances of getting the license were slim. Therefore, she asked the executive what swayed his decision. With a smile on his face, he said, "Anyone who has done such great homework as you have on my company and my personal life deserves the license."

During the preparation period, don't overlook how important it may be to spend time doing some digging for personal information on the people with whom you will be negotiating. Like the previous story shows, it may make a world of difference in the outcome. For more tips on preparing for a negotiation, see Chapter 4.

## Management/Leadership Qualities

Every successful negotiator is also an outstanding manager because negotiations are microcosms of life in the business world. We truly believe the words *negotiator* and *manager* are synonymous. After all, if you were to hear someone say, "He negotiated the turn at high speed," the message you would receive was that the driver managed the turn at high speed.

If you were to look up both *negotiator* and *manager* in a dictionary, you would find that the various definitions provided for both terms actually also define various aspects of reaching an agreement or settlement. Definitions for *negotiate* usually include the act of working with another individual in order to settle issues on a matter. And *manage* generally means to handle or control. Clearly, the two terms are quite compatible.

Actually, the processes of management and negotiation are inseparable; you cannot successfully do one without the other. And yet, it is amazing how many executives don't see themselves as negotiators; they believe they designate the negotiation tasks to others who, for example, manage contractors, buy supplies, or hire people. Generally, the only executives who we have found truly realized how important negotiating skills were to their success were those in marketing and sales departments.

We also discovered something else we didn't expect. There were many negotiators who managed the process very well when engaged in external bargaining sessions, yet they were not as effective when having to negotiate situations with subordinates or other employees. In other words, they were negotiating when managing outside their company, but managing without negotiating internally. One glaring example is that when they negotiated as agents for their company, they tended to pay more attention to what was said; they had an ability to listen to others. However, they seemed to leave those listening skills outside their company, because they often turned a "deaf ear" to what subordinate or other employees said.

To be successful, remember the dual role you must play when you sit down to negotiate. You're a negotiator who must manage well. For more on the manager's role as a negotiator, see Chapter 6.

In this section, we have highlighted quite a few important skills. They are qualities that are strongly evident in the successful negotiators we have known. While we have thus already provided a sketch of the type of person who is most effective at negotiating, there is more to add. The following section focuses on how important personality is in the negotiation business.

## HIGHLIGHTING PERSONALITY TRAITS

Now it's time to run through a list of basic adjectives that further describe the successful negotiator. We challenge you to do an honest self-evaluation as you read through the following aspects of personality. Your personality is integral to the process of negotiating. How you come across can gain you advantage or disadvantage. It's essential you recognize what aspects of personality contribute to winding up with a situation in which everybody wins.

## A Winning Demeanor

How likable are you? I don't believe there is anyone who enjoys negotiating with someone they dislike. Negotiators always look forward to dealing with a person to whom they sincerely like talking. Developing a good negotiating personality—that is, possessing amiability during negotiations—is a topic that few books on negotiating have spent much time discussing. And yet, like so many other characteristics, amiability is an important part of a successful negotiator's profile. It creates an environment in which individuals are more relaxed and trusting.

A negotiator's personality at first impression sets a trend for future work. Displaying a winning demeanor is therefore so important when negotiating with individuals for the first time. The successful negotiator is a master at using small talk to ingratiate himself with others. He has an uncanny ability to break the ice at the start of a negotiation.

At one of our seminars, an attendee wanted to know what perspective to adopt in order to be a negotiator with a winning personality. Our answer was to convince the other party that they're okay and that the two of you have certain things in common. Meeting that party on calm and common ground will break down the walls of fear, suspicion, and mistrust.

Perhaps the best example of how to be amiable when facing tension is a story involving S.I. Hayakawa, who was a wonderful writer, college professor, and former U.S. Senator. Those who knew him well all stated he was a master of small talk that made those around him comfortable. The story goes that in early 1943, after the Japanese attack on Pearl Harbor and at a time when there were many rumors concerning Japanese spies, Hayakawa had to wait several hours in a train station. He noticed the suspicious looks the other people who were waiting for the train were giving him. He later wrote, "One couple with a small child was staring at me with special uneasiness and whispering to each other." So what Hayakawa did was to use small talk in order to get acquainted with them.

Hayakawa pleasantly remarked to the husband that it was too bad the train was late on such a cold night in Wisconsin. The man quickly agreed. Then Hayakawa continued by mentioning that is must be difficult to travel with a small child, especially during winter when train schedules are so uncertain. Again, the husband agreed with him. Next, Hayakawa asked the child's age and, when he was told, responded that their child looked very big for his age. He received agreement—however, this time the words were accompanied with a faint smile on the man's face. Whatever tension existed was slowly melting as a result of Hayakawa's small talk.

After several more conversational exchanges, the man asked Hayakawa two questions: "You're Japanese, aren't you? Do you think the Japanese have any chance of winning?" And Hayakawa replied with a smile on his face, "Your guess is as good as mine. But I don't see how the Japanese, with their lack of coal, steel, and oil, can ever possibly beat an industrialized nation like the United States."

The man agreed with Hayakawa's comments and displayed genuine relief, saying, "I hope your folks aren't over there while the war is going on." The professor returned, "Yes, they are. My father and mother and two young sisters are over there." This opened up a more in-depth conversation on family ties. The man asked, "Do you ever hear from them?" Hayakawa's answer was, "How can I?"

Hayakawa later wrote that, at the moment, whatever apprehension the man had towards him vanished. The man and his wife were both sympathetic towards Hayakawa. They even invited him to dinner at their home. All of this occurred because of the brilliant scholar's simple small talk, his amiability, his openness. That's a winning demeanor.

## Sense of Humor

Another important part of a successful negotiator's personality is his willingness to have a sense of humor. Negotiating is very serious business. However, there is always room for having a laugh now and then. This is especially true at the very beginning, when a certain amount of stress exists due to not knowing what may transpire during the day. A little humor in the first few minutes might melt away any apprehension that exists.

Hank recalls such an incident at the beginning of what was anticipated to be a long, arduous, and hectic negotiation. After the introductions were concluded and all were sitting down, the chief negotiator for the other side gave all involved a very serious, even grim look. Then he said, "When you look at me you may see that I have a serious, wrinkled face. However, I have to warn you that behind it is a comedian struggling to get out." The light-heartedness diffused the tension. And then he smiled from ear-to-ear. He later demonstrated what a great sense of humor he had and used it, especially during difficult parts of the negotiation.

## Respectfulness

Respectfulness is not something we acquire by simply reading a book or attending a seminar and practicing everything recommended. It is something that each person must work on individually, day after day. But when someone has become humble yet wise enough to be respectful, he changes the atmosphere around him. He brings trust and comfort out in others as he displays trust and comfort. When negotiating, the more respectful the individuals are with each other, the closer they move towards achieving an "everybody wins" settlement. And whenever they are not respectful of each other, an atmosphere of doubt, hostility, or suspicion exists. Clearly, such feelings are obstacles to achieving your objectives.

Therefore, establishing a respectful working relationship with the negotiators on the other side is extremely important. Whenever mutual respect is firmly established, individuals are less inhibited about exploring whatever differences may exist, and it is much easier to discuss sensitive issues. Furthermore, the discussion is also less likely to lead to a defensive response.

During Hank's early years negotiating, he was a team member in a very hostile negotiation. An older and more experienced negotiator whispered in his ear, "Don't worry, they fight like cats and dogs like this all the time. But somehow they always wind up with successful agreements!" The negotiators knew each other and had already established a good deal of respect for each other. So they allowed themselves to be emotionally charged. But for most of us, being respectful means controlling emotions. Even situations in which you have great respect for the negotiators involved can be challenging; a show of impatience can give the impression that you have lost respect for your fellow negotiators. The successful negotiator strives to be even-tempered and consistent in his display of respect so that constructive relationships that have already been established remain that way.

Whenever you take exception to something said to you or about you, do so without projecting hostility or being vindictive. Showing respect consistently towards others is a sure means of gaining more self-respect. Whenever we mention this in our seminars, an attendee will ask, "Does that mean you can't sound off or take exception to what was said?" And the answer is "No! You can certainly disagree." However, there's a way to disagree and still demonstrate respect. The key is in attacking the situation rather than the individual. Express your feelings in terms of the circumstances affecting you: "I find it very discouraging that little or no progress has been made here." And avoid expressing your frustration in statements such as, "You're deliberately complicating the issues and are not displaying any cooperation!" A personal attack prompts angry and defensive responses that only add to the problems.

The manner in which we display respect for others—not only when negotiating, but also in many other areas of our lives—can be so simple that is it easily overlooked. Yet the little things are so important. For instance, it is respectful to arrive on time for meetings. This shows you follow through with what you've promised. If you want to know how important it is to keep your word, even on the small things, ask a little child what he thinks. There are a lot of parents who fail to show respect to their children when they don't fulfill simple promises they made to their children. Children never forget promises, and they will remind you just how important every word is.

Many of us are not aware that individuals often make judgments concerning our credibility and trustworthiness on the basis of what we say or do in any given situation. We tend to assume our resumes and success stories count for more than our respectful rapport with others. But a credibility problem occurs when you do or say something that is incongruous to the mental profile another person has of you. So concentrate on maintaining a consistent respectfulness at all times.

# Self-Assurance

For some negotiators, it is second nature to project what is commonly described as a "winning personality," while others find it very difficult to achieve. A major distinction between the two is the degree of self-assurance the individual has. Those who are self-assured display a sense of being at ease with themselves. They are secure in themselves and therefore relaxed in the presence of others. Self-assured individuals are not working hard at trying to cover up or compensate for insecurities that plague them.

Being relaxed makes it easier to handle difficult interpersonal relationships and problems. However, nobody is capable of making you self-assured because it is a quality that you must develop yourself. The following are two factors that can assist you in being self-assured at the next negotiation you conduct.

First, always do your homework. To begin with, it is extremely important to recognize *all* the issues and then to prioritize them from your point of view. In a negotiation, no matter is too small to consider. However, by labeling each issue—as major, minor, or unimportant, for example—you realize which ones you need to fight for and which ones you can let go. This mental organization will allow you to function more self-assuredly. You will avoid being blindsided by something you were completely unprepared to discuss. There are fewer things that will take a negotiator "off his game" than when he is unprepared. When you prepare yourself in advance, try to determine what questions will be asked and how they will be worded. That way, you will feel more confident.

Second, develop a good overview of the general situation and the attitudes that you will probably encounter. Once you have completed the close-point work of studying all the issues, turn to the bigger picture and try to anticipate the tone of the upcoming negotiation. When you've done a good job with this, you won't feel nervous or unsure when the negotiation begins and when each issue is discussed.

Of course, there is more to developing self-assurance than the above two factors. One of the fundamental foundations for it is based on being proud of what you've accomplished in your career as a negotiator—the success you've experienced. The important point to understand is that no one can give you self-esteem, only you can develop it. And it does not occur overnight; sometimes it takes an entire lifetime. However, even a novice can possess a self-assured attitude in negotiating by acknowledging that he is as worthy as the next person—no more worthy, and no less worthy. Once you have this attitude, you'll be able to handle hostility and defensiveness when you encounter them, instead of having fear or feeling insecure when attacked.

When others jab at you in their frustration and irritation, you can deftly respond with conciliatory patience. Don't forget about the person who once was called a "stupid ass." With a smile on his face, he responded, "Now that we agree on something, let's see what else we can agree on." That's a classic example of someone who is self-assured. The less confidence you have in yourself, the faster you will give up trying to win more at the negotiation. Self-assurance is the key problem for those who always seem to settle for less.

Because negotiating is a bilateral process, it's very easy to think that any difficulties in the process are caused by the other party. And it's very easy to forget that we are the other half of the process and therefore potentially contribute something to whatever problems have occurred. But the self-assured negotiator can analyze a situation quite objectively and determine his own role in and responsibility for the good and the bad. He realizes he has just as much power to mess up as the other guy does. An expression that was used years ago is actually appropriate here: "We have seen the enemy, and he is us!" Sometimes negotiators are their own enemies, and being unwilling to realize this actually stunts that negotiator's growth as a professional. A self-assured individual will not refuse to identify his own mistakes and will therefore grow in the process.

A negotiator who is self-assured recognizes the impossibility of perfection; he clearly realizes that he will make mistakes. That's the simple reason why pencils have erasers. Concerning mistakes, if we have learned anything during all our years in negotiating, it is two things. First, everyone occasionally makes mistakes. And second, if one keeps his eyes open and ears alert, he can pick up enough information to sometimes correct mistakes made.

# Self-Restraint

This trait goes hand-in-hand with the effective listening skill discussed earlier in this chapter. Give the other side the opportunity to express their feelings, thoughts, and ideas. And when playing the role of listener, remember to keep your mouth shut, even if you don't agree with what has been stated. Instead of interrupting, make a note of the area of disagreement and wait for the propitious time to respond. We believe a major mistake often made in negotiations is not allowing a person to finish his statement and totally air out how he feels or what he believes. We know that it takes a lot of self-restraint to wait until your turn, but we also know that the wait is definitely worth it.

A colleague of ours, who is not only well-known but also an excellent negotiator, believes that when someone finally "comes up for air" and has run out of words, it is an ideal time to ask a specific question on something that person has stated. Ask a question instead of responding in disagreement. This suggestion is based on a simple negotiating rule: "You will never find out what another wants, needs, or seeks unless you let them talk!" So restrain yourself from jumping to an argument. Instead, ask clarifying questions to confirm that you see the whole picture.

We have recorded hundreds of negotiations on videotape during our seminars and have discovered something very important. When you listen well to what someone says, it is amazing how well he will listen to you. Try it at your next negotiation. Practice self-restraint; hold your tongue until the other side has completed its statements. Give yourself a moment to gather your thoughts in a logical, not an emotional, way. And *then* speak.

# Frankness and Honesty

A factor that always simplifies things immeasurably, not only in a conversation with a friend but also in a very serious negotiation, is frankness. We can define frankness as displaying your feelings and thoughts honestly, instead of sugar-coating, underplaying, or even exaggerating them. Whenever a person says to you, "Tell me what you really think," they're simply using meta-talk, pointing out that you're not being open and honest with them.

Perhaps one reason why individuals are not more honest and frank when communicating a message is because it sometimes creates a momentary discomfort. However, there are times when frankness and honesty are absolutely necessary to making progress. In such cases, the manner in which to be frank yet avoid hard feelings is to preface whatever you're going to say with a little of your own meta-talk. For example, you realize the message you're about to transmit is going to have a negative impact on the person who will hear it. Therefore, you soften the message by first stating, "What I'm about to say will probably upset you, but in order to be frank and honest I have to say it." Then proceed with your response. Whenever a harsh or critical message is prefixed with a "softener," the emotional impact is always lessened.

It is likewise important to have a good sense of tact when exercising frankness. There will be times when it is more polite to hold your tongue rather than to reply frankly. We are not encouraging dishonesty here; we are simply encouraging good timing and wording. When you interject a comment that is not purposeful at the moment and only serves to upset another person, you are "speaking out-of-turn."

It is time for a final thought concerning frankness and honesty. These practices don't require you to "spill your guts." You need not disclose all of the information you have at your disposal, and you need not express all of the emotions you are experiencing. What frankness and honesty preclude is misrepresentation of facts and the deliberate misleading of other people concerning your intentions, decisions, and actions.

# Trustworthiness

During our seminars, there have been occasions when individuals expressed their opinions and feelings concerning the type of personality they most preferred when negotiating. And near the top of this list has always been a trustworthy person. Let's look at this more closely in order to better understand specifically what is meant by "someone you can trust."

In the superior-subordinate situation found in management, trust usually means delegating responsibility and authority to another person and believing that person will carry out the duties in such a manner that will satisfy the boss. To some extent the same is true in a negotiation; when it is concluded, the negotiator trusts that the other party will do exactly what it agreed to accomplish in the settlement. However, during the negotiating process, trust encompasses much more than that. It has human dimensions that are far greater and deeper. It involves believing that the other person is truthful in what he says and does. Whenever you ask a question, you want to be confident that the other party is sure in what it knows and will give you quick and direct answers without any hesitation or doubt. In other words, you "trust" the other party will not lie or in any way distort the truth. Intuitively, we know when trust exists and when it doesn't.

Trust is difficult to describe simply because it is fundamentally a belief and feeling. No doubt you have heard someone say, "I don't trust them," and when you asked why, he had no plausible or clear answer that supported his feeling. So you went ahead anyway and signed an agreement. And then afterwards you had to face those irritating "I told you so!" remarks from the person whose gut told him not to trust.

Whatever trust is, we believe it is the glue that holds a negotiation together. It is the substance that every relationship in our life needs to have. Whenever trust does not exist, the relationship does not last very long; this is especially true in a marriage. In many situations, it is very difficult to establish trust, very easy to lose it, and very difficult to regain. So proving your trustworthiness by being an honest and conscientious negotiator will make your job much easier.

# Persistence

A very important aspect of the negotiator's personality is persistence. There are times when a negotiator has to continue steadfastly under very difficult conditions and in an unfriendly environment. Having persistence will make you a better negotiator.

Whenever you read a biography of a successful individual, you always find that his success didn't occur overnight. A classic example of this found in Ray Kroc, the founder of McDonald's. He had some very poignant words to say about persistence:

Nothing in the world can take the place of persistence. Talent will not, nothing is more common than unsuccessful people with great talent. Genius will not, unrewarded genius is almost a proverb. Education will not, the world is full of educated derelicts. Persistence and determination alone are omnipotent.

Persistence is doing what former President Ronald Reagan often stated: "Staying the course." Yet it is very important to realize that persistence does not mean "bull-headedness" or "inflexibility." It does not imply the refusal to change directions when negotiating. Persistence means not losing sight of your objectives, but sometimes that includes a change in direction. A successful negotiator is open to changing directions in order to stay on course. As an old Chinese proverb wisely instructs us, "If we don't change our direction, we're likely to end up where we're headed."

During seminars conducted, we have heard many attendees exclaim that their greatest errors made in past negotiations were due to giving up too soon, not hanging in there when they should have. Had they done so, most admit the settlements they reached would have been much sweeter. They regretted giving in. So remind yourself that persistence will pay off. Most often, a healthy stick-to-it-ness will produce a more pleasing and productive result.

# Patience

Another discovery we have made is that many people who are striving to be effective negotiators don't understand that success requires patience. As the old expression states, "You can't make a good deal if you're in a hurry!" Consider a simple but effective example. A little girl asked her parents for a two-wheeled bicycle, and she was told she could not have one because she was too small to ride it. On her next birthday, her parents—who customarily measured their daughter's height—remarked, "You're growing faster than a weed!" The child waited for two more years and then, when her parents made the same comment, wisely asked, "Fast enough for a two-wheeled bicycle?" Here, a wonderful definition of patience certainly applies well: "Patience is frustration under control!"

A master chef will take time to prepare a gourmet meal without rushing through the cooking process. Similarly, a wise negotiator will not to hurry through the negotiating process. It takes time for opposing parties to overcome anxiety and replace it with feelings of cooperation and compromise. It takes time to remove doubt and replace it with trust. The path to persuasion is not suited to quick conversion. The main reason why patience is so important is because negotiations are not always as nice and neat as we would like them to be.

## Creativity

Generally speaking, expert negotiators are emotionally mature, articulate, and sophisticated people. But if truth be told, they are also childlike. Note we do not claim that successful negotiators are child-*ish*. That would be something very different. No, instead, they have the creativity of children who are excitedly processing information and figuring out solutions without the baggage and boundaries that adults typically place around themselves.

The binary computer answers questions in combinations of zeros and ones. But a child has a more subtle understanding of, and therefore way of answering, questions. In his own way he will ask, "How can I overcome this obstacle? How can I organize this information? What is related to what?" And then he'll come up with answers that are not bound by cultural guidelines or limits learned from experience. For children, magic is a given! So they are able to think outside the box.

Successful negotiators can think outside the box and come up with original, clever solutions. They make negotiating fun because they have exciting ways of looking at situations. If you'd like to review a great example of creative thinking at the negotiation table, return to Chapter 1 and the story of St. Peter's Church (see page 11). It will remind you that coming up with new solutions makes the negotiation more lively, interesting, and successful.

Now that you have finished reading this section, tally your own score. How many of these desirable characteristics do you strongly possess? Which ones would you like to enhance? Hopefully you find yourself inspired to work on several of these areas of personality.

## CONCLUSION

The art of negotiating requires each one of us to become an artist. And artists use many different colors and methods when painting. Some have great preference for certain colors and strokes, so they use them often. Similarly, every negotiator has personality traits he has been accentuating for many years—traits he relies on for success when negotiating. But a word of caution: be wary of using the same colors too often, especially when negotiating with the same individuals. Remember; those who return to the familiar are very predictable. That's why it is important to develop as many winning traits as possible, and showcase them at appropriate and varying times.

We have now completed the basic background necessary for a study of the art of negotiating. After all, we've defined and identified the fundamentals of negotiating, analyzed human behavior, and discussed what it means to be an expert negotiator. So it is time to turn to actually conducting a negotiation. It starts with some intense preparation work, and that is the topic of the next chapter.

# 4

# The Preparation Period
## Initial Steps and
## Possible Approaches

*"Start out with an ideal and end up with a deal."*

—KARL ALBRECHT

We believe that the only predictable aspect of negotiations is that they are all different. Regardless of how many times you've negotiated with the same individual(s), you can be assured that something different will occur this time around. Therefore, the proper mindset in the preparation is not to think the process will be a carbon copy of the last one. But despite the unique nature of each negotiation, there are constructive ways to prepare.

Who are the individuals who will attend? What issues are being brought to the table? What is the main need that needs to be satisfied? What initial offers will you make, and what limits will you place upon those offers? What strategies and tactics will you use in the pursuit of your own goals? Then you have to consider what you believe the other party will say and do. What needs are they seeking to satisfy? What tactics can they possibly use? It's like peeking over the fence into a neighbor's backyard to check out what's there.

Let's take a tour through the various areas involved in preparing for a negotiation. From isolating the issues to choosing the best approach, preparation is a key part of the successful negotiator's agenda. But even before a negotiator begins to take inventory of the central issues and possible outcomes, it is important for her to take an inventory of the self.

## KNOWING THYSELF

We are firm believers in the "know thyself" principle—acquiring an intimate knowledge of oneself during preparation. This involves assessing your strengths and weaknesses so that you can choose the negotiation tactics that put you in the best position. For example, you should study your emotional limits and your tendencies to react. If you are easily angered, it might be possible for the opposition to corner you into an unfavorable settlement.

Sometimes a negotiator who is emotionally reactive finds it difficult to change direction; this is when the angry child in her comes out and she loses focus, logic, and persuasiveness. We have met some expert negotiators who can get a usually mild mannered, easy-going person to lose her temper and composure. Imagine what they can do to someone prone to tension and anger! An excitable person is simply putty in their hands. "Losing it" actually makes a negotiator more vulnerable, not intimidating. Do you "lose it"?

How do you get to truly know yourself? Begin with an intimate examination of your sense of values, your philosophy and outlook on life, and your intellectual and emotional makeup. Chapter 3 started you on this journey, as it asked you to genuinely consider your talents and personality traits. Now widen the scope. Apply the wisdom offered by a well-known Shakespeare character, *Hamlet's* Polonius, who counseled his son, "To thine own self be true!"

Have the courage to ask yourself rigorous philosophical questions. What do you seek in life, outside of this particular negotiation? What is motivating you in this particular case? What are your true needs rather than what you want in the negotiation? How far are you willing to go? What boundaries do your business or personal ethics place around the upcoming negotiation?

We have often been asked by seminar attendees if it is indeed possible for someone to conduct an objective analysis of herself, and our answer is a resounding "Yes!" Your self-analysis will be a process of going from the general to the specific, which is not an easy task. Science writer Lincoln Barnett described it well when he said, "You will be trying to transcend yourself and perceive yourself in the act of perception." It is almost like a dream in which you are looking down at yourself and seeing and hearing everything that happens.

We often turn to a helpful metaphor that we heard in our own pursuits of self-analysis. The process of self-study is like sitting in a barber's chair that faces a three-way mirror. Hundreds of images of your face sweep out in a curve that stretches back to infinity. Perhaps each face in the long row is some particular aspect of your character that demands an examination. If you can ask each reflected face the correct centering question, then it will fuse with the others before it, and ultimately one complete personality will appear. And while you are accomplishing this interior inventory, you must never forget that resolving an inner conflict is the toughest negotiation. The most difficult negotiations are the ones you have with your own conscience.

In summary, before entering into a professional—or even personal—negotiation, evaluate your own value system and most fundamental goals. Examine your capacity to react to stressful situations, and begin to organize your plan so that, if you can help it, you are not put in a situation that will leave you particularly vulnerable. Establish where your ethical lines are drawn. It helps to have boundaries to work within, regarding what you consider permissible and when you consider it time to be more creative.

Finally, if you are a member of a negotiation team, you must analyze your place on the team, as well as your fellow personalities. It's difficult enough to do a self-analysis, and it's even more trying when others will be involved. In certain negotiations there will be persons attending for specific reasons: accounting, quality control, engineering, marketing research, etc. Perhaps your role will be that of chief negotiator or spokesperson. Or maybe you are a second-tier member of the team. Whatever the case, take the productive steps of assessing where you fit and how you fit with those around you.

The preparations involved in team negotiations take a much longer time to develop. Besides the discussion of the topics covered earlier in the section, you will also have to do a lot of role-playing with each individual in your party; each team member has a specific task (role) to play in the negotiation. The preparation period is the time to rehearse this role-playing and find the best team dynamic. So the team itself has to do a self-analysis. After all, the team is technically one unit made up of various parts, just like a person and her personality.

# IDENTIFYING THE ISSUES

Once you have completed a self-analysis (and, perhaps, a team analysis), it is time to forge ahead into an analysis of the upcoming negotiation. What are the issues that will be placed on the table? All the issues with which you will ever have to deal fall into two categories: the known and the unknown. So take a step back and look at all the parameters involved in the negotiation. Decide what issues are definite or known, and what issues are possible and anticipated, or unknown.

Now let's break it down further. Each known issue will fall into one of two areas: major or minor. Be sure to determine what goes where. The unknowns will be grey areas. The grey issues are those hazy ones that may or may not exist over the course of the negotiation. They sometimes take up a great amount of discussion time during the preparation period because there is fear they may become real issues at some point. These are the areas that you believe it would be foolish to assume are unimportant and require no thought or discussion whatsoever, but to discuss them takes a lot of musing and projecting.

A great mistake often occurs during preparation when we don't recognize "iceberg issues." These issues are not hidden—they are known—but are usually wrongly categorized as minor. The problem is that we underestimate their importance because they *appear* small. We only see the top of them, that portion above the water line. Many ships have sunk simply because the individual at the helm clearly saw ice ahead but failed to realize its true size and depth.

So basically, in order to prepare well for a negotiation, you must compile a list of all the issues and cluster them into the appropriate categories. The term *issues* includes needs, desires, current dynamics between people, and possible outcomes. Once you have categorized your issues, the process of researching them begins.

# RESEARCHING THE DETAILS

Investigating the issues takes a lot of research, and therefore a lot of time. A wealth of material accumulates and resides in your mind. It needs to be assembled into a cohesive outline and picture. But it is important to give yourself boundaries and impose a time limit on your research. Oftentimes, setting a limit on your research time will aid you in making optimal use of your time.

Also, research should be conducted as objectively as possible. Do your best to avoid emotional reactions and personal judgments as you unfold details. You will get more done if you keep the task in mind and your ego to the side. There are two general areas of research we can examine.

## Details on the Person

You should always be prepared to consider any kind of information about the people with whom you are going to negotiate. Former U.S. President John F. Kennedy believed in this method. When he was preparing to meet with Russian Premier Khrushchev in Vienna, Austria, he studied all of the Premier's speeches to the public and to the Politburo. Furthermore, Kennedy researched what Khrushchev preferred for breakfast, what he liked to drink, and what music he enjoyed listening to.

Obviously, you need not go to the depths that Kennedy did, but his curiosity is inspiring. And Kennedy's meticulous search for information later paid wonderful dividends. All of us can learn from his example as we conduct our next preparation. "Don't leave any leaf unturned" is the lesson! A great amount of time and effort should be spent in preparing to understand the nature and behavior of the person with whom you will negotiate. You will discover useful information and facts about them, such as hobbies and even intellectual interests. Then you might be able to find common ground on which to rely, or a way to charm that person by appealing to her likes.

Another effective method of research is to investigate any records of previous instances of litigation, lawsuits, recorded judgments, and the like. During Jerry's many years as a New York City attorney, he found such records to be a fruitful source of valuable information about individuals with whom we was going to negotiate with. You might find out about a trend in the person's behavior, a vulnerable spot, or even an issue to avoid because it will trigger bad memories or associations.

## Details on the Business History

It is essential to examine the other party's past business history, not only with you, but also with others. You need to find out that party's previous transactions and the individuals involved, plus the deals the party has failed to consummate. Such information will be very valuable at sensitive times during the negotiation.

The interesting aspect of this detective work is that you may learn more about another party from their failures than from their successes. And if you carefully analyze the reasons why a certain deal or negotiation was unsuccessful, you will learn a great deal about how that other party thinks—their methods of operating. This allows you to develop a psychological profile of them. It will give you greater insight into what makes them tick and therefore will move you more closely to a successful negotiation.

Cautions are necessary to present at this point. To insure you are not being mislead, don't rely on a single source when you are researching. Let's use a real estate example. There are agencies that you can contact that will assist you in assessing a fairly accurate number of what the previous sales price for a property was. The more sources you use, the better your estimate will be on what the current true value of the property is and what price you should offer. Conducting a process of investigating previous real estate sales also will give you a faint idea of what kind of person you will have to negotiate with. For example, you will discover how long he owned the property before deciding to sell it. And since you now know the price it sold for, you will also know the amount of profit made.

Does the process of such in-depth research sound tedious? Of course! But today's negotiators have something wonderful: the Internet. What a tremendous source of information on anything you want to discover, learn about, and link to! You can also make use of the National Data Bank, which has statistical information. Use it for purposes of making your demands and position more credible.

Don't forget to cover all areas for clues. Have you looked at available details concerning the other party's budgets and financial planning; the publicity they received in press releases; what educational material they may have circulated; their previous advertising history and reasons for any changes in it; and reports they may have made to governmental agencies? These are examples of information that would not likely be available in the company's annual report or through the business sector but that would be accessible through the Internet or conversations with company workers.

Francis Bacon was a British philosopher, writer, Attorney General, and Lord Chancellor in the late-nineteenth and early-twentieth century. He wrote an essay titled "Of Negotiating." His words are particularly poignant:

> If you would work any man, you must either know his nature and fashion, and so lead him; or his ends, and so persuade him; or his weakness or disadvantages, and so awe him; or those that have interest in him, and so govern him. In dealing with cunning persons, we must ever consider their ends, to interpret their speeches; and it is good to say little to them, and that which they look for. In all negotiations of difficulty, a man may not look to sow and reap at once; but must prepare business, and so ripen it by degrees.

In total, the characterization of the people with whom you will negotiate is necessary in order to minimize the amount of surprises you may encounter during the negotiation. The more you know, the better the show!

## CLARIFYING THE PRECONDITIONS

So you've assessed yourself, identified key issues, and accomplished in-depth research. Now what? It's finally time to start considering your specific approach to the upcoming negotiation. To do just that, you must focus on the unchangeable circumstance that will frame everything else at that table. In other words, what precondition characterizes the relationship between the parties and therefore gives shape to the negotiation tactics?

At workshops, when we first use the term *precondition for negotiating,* we seldom fail to get many confused facial expressions from the attendees. In fact, the faces nonverbally express to us that they have heard the term but don't know what it means. Simply stated, preconditions are what motivate us or prompt us to engage in the negotiation process to begin with.

Preconditions are the circumstances that govern the position in which either party stands relative to the other. Often there is such focus on the desired end of the bargaining process that those present lose sight of their actual position relative to the other party. Whenever you allow confusion to enter in here, you'll discover it is difficult to devise a manageable strategy for meeting your objectives. In the following paragraphs, we provide a number of sample preconditions so that you can better understand the importance of clarifying your precondition before going any further into the preparation process. At first you'll find many of these possible preconditions seem self-evident, but beware of dismissing further consideration of them for that reason. Remember, we want to think fully through every aspect of a negotiation.

## Needing Assistance to Solve a Problem

One possible precondition is a need for assistance in solving a situation that adversely affects you. The other party can aid you in that objective. The important thing to keep in mind is that you are the one who is experiencing the adverse effect, so you have to take the initiative. Therefore, you have to somehow negotiate with the other party to change the activity or inactivity that is troubling you, while they are existing in relative safety. The hard work of convincing will fall on your shoulders, and you must remember to be properly thankful. Your best approach is to find something that you can offer the other team that will make working with you a true perk.

## Managing a Shared Threat

Another possible precondition is a shared threat that you and the other party face from the same source. This situation differs from the previous one in that both of you need to find a solution to a problem; the problem affects both sides in the same manner. And you have both agreed that the best approach is a cooperative effort for purposes of achieving success. Motivating your partner is less at issue here than agreeing on the mechanics of cooperation. Thus, your strategy should be should be to build on your common interests.

## Gaining an Advantage

Next, imagine that the precondition is a possible chance to gain something. You want to check out whether there is an opportunity that will benefit you. This type of negotiation allows a negotiator considerable flexibility because there's no particular urgency attached to the process and no critical issue. It isn't unusual in such cases to find that both parties share the same precondition. And considering the fact that you have nothing to lose and maybe something to gain, you will not be in an adversary position. This often contributes a positive feeling to the whole experience. The one thing you must guard against is deceiving yourself concerning the possible gains. Here, you don't want to inflate possibilities.

## Looking for Favor

A very common precondition is the desire for influential favor—you want the other party to become favorably disposed to your interests. You seek to develop some kind of assurance that the other party will use its influence on your behalf when dealing or talking to a third party. This is exactly what takes place on a daily basis in Washington, D.C., politics. That's what makes the dynamics involved in lobbying activities.

## Selling a Product or Service

Let's not forget about the precondition of a sales opportunity when you're selling a product or service. Your first step is to develop a need in the other party for a product or service you can provide.

Simply stated, selling is the process of motivating others to buy. So in this situation you first have to spend time probing the other side's circumstances and attitudes. And then you have to convince the other party that employing your product or service will result in their personal improvement.

There's more to say on the whole process of selling. The most important aspect in the selling process is maintaining your credibility. And if you can lay a finger on an experienced want or need but are unable to close the deal, it's because your precondition of credibility has not been satisfied. Above all others in the field of negotiating, salespeople develop an ability to read others, to know when to emphasize a point and when to remain silent. And they must always conduct themselves so that the focus of the negotiation remains on how they can provide the best answer to the needs of the other party.

## Purchasing a Product or Service

Now switch gears and imagine the precondition is buying. You want someone to provide a product or service in order to fulfill one of your own needs. The first thing to do in this situation is to clearly communicate your needs and desires. And when you've accomplished that, you must ascertain whether or not the other party is capable of satisfying those needs and desires. The reason why this is so important to emphasize is that, in some instances, the other party is actually unable to provide exactly what you need, yet they are eager to sell to you. Remain fixed to your original needs; resist the temptation to adjust your needs to the product being offered just so that you can close the deal.

When the precondition involves buying, it is a huge mistake to allow the mindset that only one party can satisfy you. If you look further, you might discover there are other sources of products as well—products that more appropriately fulfill your needs. Be wise and avoid falling into this mental trap in which your bargaining advantages are very limited.

## Renegotiating a Contract

A very typical precondition is a contract *re*negotiation, which occurs when an original contract or agreement will shortly expire. This type of precondition often brings labor and management to the negotiating table. It also applies to situations in which executives will negotiate with board members on tenure and employment conditions spelled out in a contract. The tactics appropriate in these circumstances will vary considerably.

If both parties truly want to renew, then the negotiation should be characterized by an immediate sense of mutual interests and there will be very little conflict. However, in some labor-management negotiations, both sides get so involved in their respective tactics that the atmosphere and environment of working together to satisfy mutual interests actually is harmed. Each side gets so caught up in achieving intermediate goals and devising tactics to win that mutual interest recedes into the background and is sometimes totally forgotten. This is evident when the parties exchange recriminations that push them further apart than when they started to negotiate. There are occasions when we read of companies going out of business simply because their labor negotiations became severely acrimonious and resulted in a "lose-lose" ending.

## Disengaging a Business Relationship

A very interesting precondition is when we have a desire to disengage a business relationship that has existed for either a short or long time. Perhaps most of us may think that such a circumstance doesn't require a negotiation—the service arrangements with someone simply have proven to be unsatisfactory or no longer necessary. We believe that, in some instances, the relationship can easily and cleanly terminate just by giving notice. However, in actuality, this precondition makes negotiation necessary in many cases. If you're dissolving a formally established business partnership, you'll find you must come to an agreement on the disposition of assets or on responsibility for debits that may remain.

Whenever you have the precondition of disengaging a relationship, the negotiation is less likely to focus on the dissolution itself than on the manner of its accomplishment. The argument will center on who contributed the most to the success of the business and therefore deserves "the lion's share." That's an issue that most other types of negotiations seldom have to resolve, and it's a very ugly process when the egos clash.

Dissolving relationships are often characterized by very hard feelings on one or both sides, and the negotiations can quickly become very vindictive and acrimonious. This is especially true in business and in divorce settlements. Perhaps there is some satisfaction achieved in seeing someone who has become "the enemy" suffer. Unfortunately, such mean-spirited behavior in this kind of circumstance creates victims on both sides.

## Salvaging a Relationship

What about when the relationship breaks down and you are trying to salvage it? In the tenuous dynamic of a floundering relationship, the wrong words or actions can set you farther from your objectives than when you started. Perhaps this is one of the most delicate situations a negotiator can face. Unless the bargaining is conducted with considerable tact, the risk of not meeting the precondition is very great. The situation is extremely sensitive because you have to deal with the specific issues that have contributed to the deterioration of the relationship without getting hung up in a defensive or fact-finding conflict.

In such situations, we suggest that you be prepared beforehand to acknowledge your own responsibility and contribution to the condition. For example, if you are a temperamental boss faced with the threatening departure of a very valuable employee who finds the manner in which you exercise your authority hard to take, you must avoid a response that is full of authority. Replace it with one that communicates understanding and sensitivity. Above all, don't let your ego dominate.

One precondition we have all faced at least once in our lifetime is the "last-ditch salvage effort." This is a situation in which we want to save whatever we possibly can at all costs. And it becomes even more difficult whenever the other person has the upper hand and we have little or no leverage. In order to handle this situation, we suggest that you consider the other person's preconditions—especially her needs.

Ultimately, you can't bargain for assistance if no one is interested in your problem; you can't sell if no one wants to buy; you can't save your job if no one is open to persuasion. However, everyone, in every situation, has needs. The needs that are most universal are "ego needs." We have discovered that approaching each situation, regardless of what the preconditions may be, with the other person's ego needs in mind has merit. Therefore, prepare for your negotiations by considering the other person's ego needs. There will be times when doing so works better than others, but whenever you make that effort, the strategy always produces some sort of positive effect.

## APPLYING NEED THEORY

Once the defining precondition is established, your next step will be to hone in on a specific approach. We have done something very unique in order to help you do just that. During his years as a professional negotiator, Jerry realized that Abraham Maslow's work on basic needs, discussed in Chapter 2, could wonderfully apply to the art of negotiation. Originally, that work was devised to help explain aspects of human psychology, but Jerry saw the kernels of something more.

## The Development of Need Theory

If people had all their needs satisfied, they would never have to negotiate. The very premise of a negotiation is that the individuals who are involved in it want to get something. This is true even if the need is simply to maintain the status quo. So a negotiation requires two or more parties who seek to gain something and are motivated by their needs. Whether we are discussing husband/wife negotiations, parent/child negotiations, the sale of real estate, a business contract, a proposed merger, or any other negotiation, in every instance, there are needs to be fulfilled.

Maslow's work shows us that needs can be categorized and prioritized, and should be done so according to each individual. If we insert negotiation terms into the statement, we find that each party has a particular list of needs that can be arranged from most dire to least concerning. The needs of a party should be assessed before, during, and after a negotiation. This focuses our attention and allows us to plan and use alternative methods for satisfying those needs. It also guides us on how to react to whatever tactic the other party may use.

So Jerry took Maslow's approach and formulated a Need Theory for negotiating. It teaches us to arrange the needs that are involved in an effective order according to their importance in both parties' lives. When we are aware of the relative strength and power of each need, we are then able to decide on the method to use in dealing with it.

Need Theory is applicable at all levels of negotiating, for all levels of management, and in every organization. The theory includes six different negotiating styles:

1. Negotiating for another's needs

2. Giving no assistance and making the opposing party negotiate for its own needs

3. Negotiating for both sides' needs, especially those which are common

4. Negotiating against your own needs

5. Negotiating against another's needs

6. Negotiating against both sides' needs

In every single negotiation we have ever conducted, we applied one or more of the above styles during the course of the bargaining session. If truth be told, most of the time we were guilty of being unaware of precisely what we were doing at the time. But the art of negotiating involves becoming aware of the styles we use and the opposing side uses during the entire course of the negotiation. Need Theory is a great map that charts our course and direction. Let's look at the approached more specifically.

## Negotiating for Another's Needs

This approach refers to when the negotiator makes efforts to persuade, assure, coax, back, or champion the other side. Why would a negotiator do so? So that he could free his party of certain fears, whether those fears concern financial security, emotional well-being, or some other area of interest. So the main approach is to feed the ego of the other side and hope that party responds in an amicable, amenable way to your goals.

## Giving No Assistance

In this approach, the negotiator challenges, incites, spurs on, or stimulates the other party to pursue its needs by not giving much at the get-go. She doesn't work to lay common ground in front of the other party. Similarly, the negotiator doesn't use the "I'll scratch your back if you scratch mine" tactic. This is a simple approach that demands, "Show me what you have, and I'll respond accordingly. Until then, I'm going to remain firm and silent."

## Negotiating for Both Needs

Years ago, serious racial rioting broke in several East Coast cities. The residents of Newark, New Jersey, fully expected the same thing would occur in their city because it had a large black population, poverty, poor housing, and a great deal of discontent. However, to their surprise, there was no disturbance and the city's citizens wanted to know why.

The reason is rooted in the fact that the mayor of Newark had made it a practice to keep in close contact with the leaders of the black community at all times. He made frequent visits to the Central Ward, a potential trouble spot. And through his consultation with religious and civic leaders, he was fully informed of the mood in the black community and aware of whatever grievances existed there. With many riots flaring in neighboring cities, all Newark needed was a spark that would ignite a riot in that city. So careful monitoring was conducted.

Therefore, when a group outside the city decided to hold a rally in a predominately black section of the city, the Mayor realized he had to do something quickly in order to head-off any troubles. He wired telegrams to more than ninety community leaders, and within hours most of them were in his office discussing action that needed to be taken. The results produced actually turned the proposed rally from a potential riot into a peaceful drive for black voter registration.

The mayor's actions were successful because he worked for both sides—the continued safety and spirit of the community, and the individuals' need to make their presence heard and belong to a strong group. If the mayor had worked against such needs by banning the rally, it would have, without doubt, led to an emotional display, violence, and a riot. This type of approach involves recognizing, emboldening, and cooperating.

## Negotiating Against Your Own Needs

Children at a very young age intuitively know how to work against their homeostatic needs—they hold their breath while negotiating with parents for a certain new toy or something else they want. Some wise parents wait until the child gets blue in the face and then watch her take a long breath of air in order to continue living. Others cave in to the child's demands and buy the toy or whatever it is she wants. The tactic is not always successful, but it is an example of working against one's own needs.

In negotiating, this approach can involve waiving certain advantages, sacrificing perks, recanting previous statements, yielding to another's pressure, or even forgoing a desire. But the gain would be greater than the loss. In the political arena, the situations of ceasefires and pacifistic acts are examples of this type of approach.

## Negotiating Against Another's Needs

When a negotiator works against the opposer's needs, she is taking a road that could lead to a very charged and antagonistic environment. But sometimes that is necessary. There is no room for flattery or even support and acknowledgment with this approach. It involves aggressive moves, such as prohibitions, vetoes, hindrances, and even threats. It's a "me against you" avenue.

Sometimes this approach can get truly ugly, especially when it involves betrayals, harassments, and abuses. In its extreme form, negotiating against another's needs includes sabotage and true misuse of power. While this is rarely the road we'd suggest, it has its place among the myriad of possibilities when it comes to negotiation strategies.

## Negotiating Against Both Sides' Needs

Once during a seminar an attendee asked, "How in the world would a tactic of working against both sides ever succeed?" In response, we gave the following example. In Japan many years ago, the train conductors went on strike. However, they did a very unusual thing—they all showed up for work the following day on schedule and worked the entire day for no pay whatsoever. It wasn't until the end of the workday that the transport company discovered something very surprising. Although the workers had performed their duties, they had not collected any fares. Therefore, there was no income for the organization. The workers worked against both needs—their own needs for payment in return for their services, and the company's need to collect revenue through fares.

Another example we gave was the time when the shoemakers in Italy went on strike. The first day of their strike, instead of picketing or staying at home, they all returned to their workstations and manufactured shoes. Management was completely surprised and shocked at their behavior and decided not to take any action or ask any questions. At the end of the day the supervisors inspected the work that had been accomplished. It was then they received their second big surprise: the workers had only produced shoes for the left foot. Therefore, they had a large number of shoes that could never be sold. It did not take the management much longer to realize they had better negotiate a settlement with the workers, which they did the following day.

These are very clear examples of how working against the needs of both sides can actually produce results. In international dealings, this is where negotiations on armament reduction would often fall. So too would situations that are characterized by "separate but equal."

So now you understand how Need Theory works. The negotiator evaluates the situation and chooses one of the styles detailed in this section. When discussing Need Theory with a friend of ours, she quickly associated it with a process that is followed by commercial airline pilots. She stated, "During a flight, the senior pilot has to be aware of everything that is occurring in a cockpit in order to make any necessary changes or decisions in a split second. That sounds exactly like the Need Theory."

Her insightful analogy was completely correct. When an airline pilot is unaware of what is occurring during a flight, there is always a great possibility it may lead to serious consequences. The lack of attention may ultimately result in the loss of life and/or damage to the aircraft. Like a pilot, a negotiator has to constantly monitor many things—some that are said and some that are simply occurring. That means full-time awareness and staying alert at the controls! It means adjusting tactics to the needs of the moment and prioritizing effectively.

## GENERATING IDEAS WITH A TEAM

In addition to traditional methods of preparation, such as doing your homework and examining records, there are others you may wish to use. They include conferencing, brainstorming, and psychodrama. These methods, originally used by psychologists and by advertising agencies, have proven to be valuable in generating creative ideas. And as we have emphasized before, creativity makes a negotiation much more likely to be successful and much more fun.

Brainstorming, conferencing, and psychodrama can all be used when you are attempting to predict what the other party is going to demand, say, do, and compromise on. The use of group dynamics had proven to be a highly effective way to get answers to such questions. Group interaction in solving problems is powerful; it often generates more suggestions, feedback, and responses that are not only critical but also creative and more plentiful than one individual would develop alone. Solving problems through a group judgment has often proved to be superior to results obtained by individual judgments. This is especially true to the advertising profession.

## Conferencing

The method called conferencing is very simple. It is used, for example, when an organization is seeking a slogan for a new product or service. The usual procedure is to schedule a conference for the purpose of generating opinions and ideas. Each member of the group comes to the meeting equipped with a few good ideas. The ideas are presented in an orderly fashion and then weighed against each other. Finally, a decision is made based on the consensus reached regarding the most effective idea.

## Brainstorming

Brainstorming is similar to conferencing, but less organized, more spur-of-the-moment. A group of team members gets together and verbally tosses around any ideas that come to mind. Everything said is recorded. There is no constraint on whatever individuals think or say; the focus of the brainstorming session may stray in any direction, as participants say anything that pops into their minds. It is a very liberal, creative atmosphere in which there are no "do's or don'ts." When the conference is concluded, the recording will be given to executives who will evaluate the ideas and make a final decision on the approach to be used.

After a great amount of research involving the analytical study of the brainstorming technique, the belief is that the reason it works is because brain activity in groups becomes infectious; ideas seem to increase as a result of the mental exercise. It was also found that the non-threatening, informal atmosphere of the group not only made individuals feel secure but also relieved their inhibitions. Furthermore, the individual's creative thinking is quickened and more ideas are obtained when the pressure of a more formal and structured conference mode is not present.

## Psychodrama

The third preparation method is related to group psychotherapy, which originated with the father of psychoanalysis, Sigmund Freud, and has had many refinements since its inception. More than forty years ago, J.L. Moreno made significant improvements in its application by using groups of individuals to "play act" for purposes of solving problems. He named the process *psychodrama*. Since that time, psychiatrists use it to bring out patients' hidden feelings, attitudes, frustrations, and deepest emotions in a manner that does not cause them to feel any sense of shame or fear of ridicule.

Psychodrama, which involves role-playing, can be used in many circumstances. Let's consider two very different examples. Before canonizing a saint, the Roman Catholic Church traditionally appoints a "devil's advocate," who is instructed to advance all the arguments and reasons why the person should not be canonized. And in high school football, during practice sessions before games, coaches select individuals to role-play certain players of the opposing team. Those individuals will attempt to find flaws in whatever game plans have been made. There are many games played on Saturday during the football season that were actually won on the practice field the week before.

If you choose to use the psychodrama method, we recommend that selected individuals take the role of the other party with whom you will negotiate. That will help you to anticipate what may occur during the actual bargaining session and present it in a more vivid manner than simply talking about perceived conduct. Another benefit of psychodrama is that it may reveal some elements that you have overlooked or ignored. And it allows you to put yourself in the other person's position and view issues from that perspective.

Yet the most powerful benefit of these group dramas is that they offer an environment for self-analysis that a conference does not. A study of your own motivation and thinking often gives you clues to the probable perceptions and actions of the other side. It allows you to ask yourself exactly what you want from the forthcoming negotiation. And a thorough examination of this question will serve to clarify your thinking on acceptable solutions to the problems and situations you are going to handle.

We hope this section has given you some new ideas that will enhance your preparation practices. The methods we have discussed apply to team playing, so they are most suitable for those who are working on negotiation teams. But if you are working alone, you can still take aspects of these methods and apply them to your individual preparation period. Allow us to explain how.

Perhaps you can conference with someone you respect and who is not involved at all in the upcoming negotiation. Casually trade ideas and get her opinion on some of your plans. A new, objective opinion might prove to be very helpful. Or allow yourself the time, space, and creativity to brainstorm behind closed doors. Write down everything that comes to mind and see what your most unabashed self comes up with! Lastly, you can always do role-playing on your own, in your own mind. That's what we so often refer to as "imagination"! Humans have the unmatched ability to put themselves in other people's shoes. So project yourself into the other party's position and run through a role-play in your mind. As the other party, what are you thinking? How are you tempted to react? What are your biggest concerns?

## CONSIDERING AGREEMENTS-IN-PRINCIPLE

Something you should save until the end of your preparation, and something many negotiators seldom discuss, is agreements-in-principle. When properly used in a negotiation, they are the foundation on which you construct a base capable of withstanding the greatest amount of conflict and turbulence that may result. An agreement-in-principle is something that both sides agree is very important and necessary to their mutual relationship. It is a strong belief that neither side questions. And it should be stated early in your negotiation for purposes of returning to it when "the going gets tough." Agreements-in principle have saved our negotiations from falling apart on numerous occasions. And they should be used more often.

For example, the infamous 2007-2008 writers' union strike wrecked havoc on the world of entertainment. Although many books have been written on the subject of negotiations, none has ever mentioned the origin of the word *strike*. It originated in 1768, when British sailors backed their refusal to work by striking (lowering) the sails on ships.

In the case of the writers' strike, work on many television shows, films, and stage plays came to a grinding halt for weeks. The negotiators on both sides should have started by reaching an early agreement-in-principle that there would not be a walkout that would negatively affect their mutual "bread and butter." There is plenty of evidence from the past that whenever audiences are deprived of certain programs, they manage to find other sources of entertainment. When the strike was finally settled in February 2008, to the dismay of both sides it was discovered that box office revenues would continue to drop in the subsequent months. As for television shows, the number of viewers significantly diminished for a considerable duration, especially regarding the late-night talk shows on which people rely for comedic commentary of the most current events.

Tim Goldman, a newspaper entertainment writer, did an excellent job in his analysis of the "lose-lose" ending to the negotiation. He started his column by stating, "The Writers Guild of America may find out very soon that even if their members 'won,' they also lost." Mr. Goldman further went on to outline the disastrous results: (1) both the current season and the next would be negatively affected; (2) as a result of the strike, some writers would receive "pink slips"; (3) the cost of getting production back up would be very expensive because momentum had been lost; (4) both sides now were looking at a bleak picture for next season; (5) there would be a smaller pool of shows available for that season and some series would be shelved until 2009; (6) some programs would be cancelled and others would be cut back drastically; (7) the writers would learn what the expression, "Winning the battle, but losing the war," truly meant. After the strike was ended, it was estimated that the entertainment industry and the writers paid a total of $2.4 billion in cost.

When agreements-in-principle are clearly stated and agreed upon early in the negotiation, they may prove to be figurative life-savers. They are especially useful at times when one or both sides are seriously considering walking out of the negotiation. As always, consider your words and phrasing carefully as you shape the agreements-in-principle. Moreover, maintain the ethics to stick to those agreements. Otherwise, your credibility will dissolve.

# CONCLUSION

We have covered a lot of material on the preparation period. After reading this chapter, you might feel a little overwhelmed by the amount of energy that thorough preparation requires. But realize that a lot of it comes naturally to you. You probably already do some form of self-analysis when mentally preparing yourself for a negotiation. And you probably don't realize how often you are isolating issues, conducting research, weighing preconditions, and selecting the best negotiation approach out of several in hand. But by deeply thinking about the steps of preparation and becoming more aware of what you are actually doing, you will also notice the places where improvement is possible.

It is always wise to remember that some negotiations will have short-term implications, some will have long-term implications, and some will have both. One of the common mistakes negotiators make is being "short-sighted," which they later regret when having to face the consequences. Good preparation reduces the amount of short-sightedness. And good preparation leads to great strategies and tactics, which is the topic of our next chapter.

# 5

# Effective Negotiating Techniques

## From Selecting Strategies to Side-Stepping Impasses and Assumptions

*"It's not what you do that works; it's how you do it!"*

After many years of our combined negotiating experiences, and hundreds of seminars conducted worldwide that were attended by thousands of negotiators, we are thoroughly convinced that the above expression sums up our thoughts concerning whatever strategies or tactics you may choose to use when negotiating. Every high-school football player is told by his coach, many times before the game on Friday night or Saturday afternoon, "No matter how much we have worked on our game plan this week, the most important factor is how well you execute it!" And it is exactly the same for every negotiation you will ever spend time developing techniques for. Whatever success you will achieve is directly related to how well you handled and executed the many things planned.

Once you have set your goals set, it is time to select techniques. This chapter discusses some of the most effective techniques out there. It also offers quite a few ways to handle an impasse if those techniques aren't getting you very far. Finally, this chapter covers the dangers of hidden assumptions, because assumptions might be the very reason why generally effective techniques aren't producing progress. Yet before we delve into any of these topics, let's briefly explore the issue of power, so that you can choose your techniques wisely and practically.

# ANALYZING POWER STRUCTURE

Your choice of strategies is always dependant on power dynamics. You will choose a strategy according to how much power you hold, or think you hold, at the negotiating table. Obviously, strategy and tactics both work much better when the perception of power is on your side. When needs are very much unbalanced and the other party needs you more than you need them, you are set up for a win. However, in such situations you must be very careful not to abuse your power. If you do, the other party will never forget it and will seek revenge in a future negotiation in which power is more equally divided.

Importantly, you must realize that the other side might not perceive the power dynamics in the same way you do. Despite whatever power you may think you have, the other party might not think you are in a particularly powerful position at all. We have known many individuals who didn't understand this fundamental principle of negotiating and had to learn it the hard way! Furthermore, as negotiators, we must also be aware of what Alfred Adler wrote concerning how humans are constantly striving to raise themselves from inferior to superior positions. Power dynamics are fragile and emotional things. But where does power come from?

A source of power that almost everyone is aware of is knowledge and authority. And the negotiator who knows how to benefit from it enjoys the driver's seat. In our society, there are certain professions that inherently carry a certain amount of authority or power: doctors, lawyers, engineers, scientists, top executives, police officers, and government authorities. These professionals usually always begin negotiations in a power position due to their expertise and/or authority. How many of you have ever negotiated yourself out of a speeding ticket?

Another source of power is the title or the organizational position of a person. For example, the chief executive of an insurance firm sent one of his young adjusters to settle and negotiate a sizeable fire damage claim filed by one of the company's most prestigious clients. The young adjuster was unable to reach a settlement with the client even though the offer was more than generous. When the executive was advised, he telephoned the client to find out why she rejected the offer. She told him; "The offer wasn't bad at all, but it seems to me that considering how much business we have done in the past, you might have sent one of your more senior men to handle the matter. A vice president at least!"

Whether we like it or not, titles do carry weight, although *why* they do still remains a mystery. If you are in a managerial position, you should consider this the next time you send someone to represent you in a very important negotiation. If necessary, have new business cards printed with the latest and most applicable titles, solely to impress others. And have very high executives sent to handle the negotiation for you.

Information is a third source of power. As opposed to knowledge, the obtaining of information involves gathering data from many sources for a specific purpose. This is especially powerful when a negotiation reaches a point at which you are able to use data because the timing is perfect. Many of us can remember being jolted with fear during a negotiation when someone said, "I'm sure you're aware that . . ." and then revealed information about which we had absolutely no knowledge and which blindsided us. The party who is prepared with information has an edge on the power dynamics.

Of course, lastly and frustratingly enough, money is power. In many negotiations, the party who enjoys financial prosperity usually doesn't have to work so hard to get their demands met. Not every negotiation involves money, or even a clearly advantaged party. However, financial prowess is a common enough source of power to warrant mention here.

Certainly, power dynamics can be very complex. We have pointed out several of the sources of power simply to alert you to how important it is to think through the power issues in your upcoming negotiation. Who has the most leverage? Upon what is that leverage based? Do you have an edge when it comes to information? Should you showcase your knowledge and therefore gain a power position? These are just a few of the many questions you will benefit from asking yourself as you select negotiation techniques. Once you assess the power dynamics, you are better able to choose the most appropriate tactics.

## STUDYING STRATEGIES AND TACTICS

Now it's time to turn to a number of time-tested negotiating techniques that, if chosen wisely, can really work for you and your team. The ones we discuss are extremely varied. We hope you find yourself motivated to try a few new ones, as negotiators who are willing to take risks and tackle the unfamiliar tend to be more creative and more successful.

# Forbearance

Sometimes forbearance, referred to as "waiting in haste," requires a great amount of patience in order to work well. And age is a great teacher. Seldom will you see this strategy used by young negotiators who are in a hurry to get things done as quickly as possible. The circumstances and elements involved in the use of this strategy are capable of provoking anger, frustration, and impetuous action. But when used properly, the rewards are great.

Someone who practices forbearance holds his tongue despite temptation to react. Sometimes one party will intentionally provoke the other in order to distract that team or throw it off kilter. Quite differently, sometimes a party will enthusiastically offer to fulfill 90 percent of the other party's requests in hopes that the opposition will be charmed by the thought of resolution and go for a settlement. Forbearance is a great response in either case, for it involves a patient, self-controlled withholding of reaction until further thought can be given to the situation.

Your personality, judgment, and value systems should be considered before using forbearance, for it is challenging to accomplish and takes much stamina. Practicing forbearance involves allowing a certain amount of time to pass. Even the most experienced and professional negotiator who has used the strategy effectively in the past may forego using it simply because urgency is involved. So the situation has to be right.

Forbearance is effectively used by the Quakers, a religious organization, during meetings when they are divided in reaching agreement. At such times, they will declare a period of silence before continuing. And afterwards, if the matter is still unsettled and a division still exists, the clerk postpones the question and assigns it to be discussed at another meeting. As you are probably thinking, this process might possibly continue for a longer duration than planned. However, what it does achieve is acknowledgement of direct conflict and disagreement, as well as the hopes for eventual resolution.

Former President Franklin Roosevelt enjoyed telling a story about the Chinese use of forbearance based on four-thousand years of civilization. Two workers were arguing in the middle of a crowd of people. A foreigner expressed surprise that no blows were struck. His Chinese friend explained, "The man who strikes first admits that he no longer has any more ideas!"

## Silence

Silence is powerful. During our seminars, we ask attendees to share what strategies and tactics they prefer. Looking back on all the information we have received from them, the most often mentioned response is silence. There's something about silence that demonstrates self-control, confidence, discipline, and calm. And if you can appear to be gifted with those characteristics, you will be considered a gifted negotiator.

An attendee once said, "What has worked very well with us for many years is to say as little as possible and force the other side to convince and sell to us!" Indeed, one of the greatest mistakes often made is talking too much. Most successful negotiators are not only great speakers but also great listeners. They know that in order to persuade others and ultimately sell ideas, concepts, and things, there must be a healthy balance of talk and silence. Whether we're revealing too much or grating against the other party's nerves by being too verbose, words can sometimes become our worst enemies. So successful negotiators know that silence is just as important as talking.

In order for silence to work, the negotiator has to know when to stop talking and when to start talking. He must not undermine his position with too many words, but he also must not undermine it with too much aloofness. This is especially important when he has already achieved his objective and the thought is that he can possibly get "a little bit more." In such cases, the wisdom of Benjamin Disraeli should be considered: "Next to knowing when to seize an advantage, the most important thing in life is to know when to forego an advantage." Negotiators who understand this will seldom lose what they have gained.

## Surprise

This strategy involves a sudden shift in whatever course you may have taken. It is swift, drastic, and even emotionally dramatic. However, it doesn't have to involve a loud, high energy shift. The surprise actually can simply be lowering the tone of your voice and speaking much more slowly, with greater word emphasis. The idea is to make yourself less predictable so that the other party doesn't get too confident in their assumptions and demands.

Hank recalls someone he worked for in the aerospace industry who normally spoke loudly and rapidly. When this man was "dressing someone down" and very, very angry, instead of booming even more loudly, he would speak slowly and lower his voice. This would surprise the other party—throw them off. The other side was geared up to fight, yet this man would catch them off guard and calmly pressure them.

So when someone pushes your emotional "hot buttons" in the hopes of making you lose control, why not surprise him? When he attempts to get you angry, react like a judo expert. Don't oppose him, but work with him, using his energy to your advantage. It is possible to disarm even the most hostile individual in a negotiation with a faint smile on your face and a lowering of your voice.

## Fait Accompli

In some situations this technique may be risky because it forces you to act and then to wait and see what the response may be. In other words, fait accompli involves offering or declining something—whatever the case may be—in the hopes that the other party will react desirably to your move. It would be wise to first appraise what the consequences might be if it should fail. This technique could also be called "taking a chance."

An interesting illustration of the *unsuccessful* use of the strategy was the attack by England, France, and Israel upon Egypt during the Suez crisis. They acted without prior consultation with the United States and hoped to present to the world with a "fait accompli," or accomplished fact. To those countries' dismay, the United States intervened and forced them to abandon the attack and withdraw. The example proves that fait accompli is risky, and if the climate isn't right, it could cause much embarrassment. So use this technique prudently.

## Bland Withdrawal

Bland withdrawal is perhaps one of the strategies we learn very early in life, when our parents catch us doing something we are not supposed to be doing. We say, "Who, me?'" and we hope that the persona of innocence will somehow make them question their accusations, or put them in a position where they have to explain things further. Most people never grow out of that urge to deny something in the tension of the moment. The same reaction is still used by adults when caught red-handed. In negotiations, this approach can be used primarily to stall.

Using the bland withdrawal forces the other side to give you more information. You could use a phrase such as, "Can you explain exactly what you feel our motivation is here?" And during the process of their response, you have time to plan your next move. In some negotiations this strategy works extremely well, especially when someone attempts to pin something on you. Admitting guilt immediately deprives you of the advantage.

## Apparent Withdrawal

Whenever this strategy is used there is mixture of forbearance, self-discipline, and deception involved. The strategy is an attempt to convince the other person that you have withdrawn, when actually you haven't. The hope is that the other team will scramble to keep you in the negotiations.

Jerry used this approach once in litigation with the Rent Commission of the City of New York. The Commission determined that a hearing be scheduled, but that hearing would ultimately prove to be detrimental to Jerry's client, a landlord. The Commission agreed with Jerry's claim that his client would be disadvantaged. When the issue was taken to the Supreme Court in the state, the Court suggested to the Rent Commission that it should postpone the hearing.

In spite of the request of the Court, the Rent Commission went ahead with the hearing. Jerry attended the hearing, but before it began, he had the official stenographer take down a statement for the record in which he warned everyone in attendance that the hearing was begin held against the wishes of the Supreme Court. In addition, Jerry also advised them that he would see to it that the Court was informed about the hearing. And then, once he had advised them, walked out of the room putting "the icing" on his apparent withdrawal strategy.

What the hearing officer of the Rent Commission didn't realize was that an associate of Jerry's remained in the hearing room, seated with a group of witnesses that had been called. Prior to the hearing, Jerry and his associate had decided that the associate would take over in the event that the Rent Commission chose to go ahead with the hearing. His strategy worked perfectly because the individual in charge of the hearing was unsure of how to proceed. After some thought, he called the Rent Commission for advice, and he was told to adjourn the meeting. As a result of this, afterwards the Commission was persuaded that landlords are members of the community, and therefore, no one can be victimized without causing harm to everyone.

## Reversal

"You can go forward by going backward." When using this strategy, you act in opposition to what may be considered to be the popular trend or goal. Let's look at a financially based example. Bernard Baruch once said that people who make money in the stock market are those who are the first in and the first out. By this he meant that successful investors usually buy when everyone is pessimistic and sell when the prevailing atmosphere is optimistic. Sounds backwards, right? But it works.

The strategy of reversal may sound easy to execute, but in reality it is extremely difficult. Timing has to be perfect. Technically, the power dynamics must shift for reversal to work. The skilled negotiator knows when that's possible and when it's not. Were this approach not so difficult, we would all immediately take advantage of it and become successful at our goals, whether for wealth, prestige, or the like.

Interestingly enough, modern methods of communication have caused a reverse in many traditional negotiating roles. So this technique sometimes happens automatically. For example, Jerry once had occasion to accompany a coffee buyer on a trip to the Amazon jungle. During the trip, Jerry asked the individual if he had a special method of negotiating when purchasing coffee in that part of the world. The man laughed at Jerry and replied, "The most remote tribes in the Amazon that gather coffee beans have shortwave radios. And they get the latest prices from the New York Coffee Exchange. They then add the cost of transportation, allow a small handling charge, and tell the buyer the price he has to pay." One would think the tribes would be concerned with compromising in order to make a sale, but they figured out how to be on top when it came to power dynamics. They performed a reversal of power.

Reversal often involves changing the course of action you've taken at prior times. Sometimes it works extremely well, as it did for the American Labor Party (ALP) shortly after World War II. They had entered a candidate in the Democratic primary in a district, and there was a strong possibility that the candidate might unseat the incumbent Senator who had refused to accept their endorsement. The Senator and his staff decided to use a strategy of reversal by threatening to take over the Labor Party by entering their own candidate in the primary. And to make their threat real, they sent out squads of workers and in two days gathered enough signatures from residents of the district to challenge the ALP-sponsored candidate. At that point, the "white flag" went up and the ALP agreed not to challenge the incumbent Senator. The strategy worked as planned.

# Probing/Testing

Perhaps the most common tactic is one in which a person attempts to acquire additional information. Questions that pose hypotheticals, pry for more details, and seek deeper clarification are the stuff that probing/testing is made of. This strategy can help you to identify the other party's goals, areas of possible compromise, and limits. The trick is not to make yourself sound too unstable, and not to inflame the other party by digging too deeply. This, perhaps, is one of the most important tactics when used properly, because in many instances, it narrows the distance between the negotiators.

There are many expressions that verbally pave the way for the use of probling/testing. Consider several examples: "In order to better understand . . ."; "What if . . ."; "In the event of . . . ." All of these phrases seek a response that will give the inquirer a broader vision of what the other party wants, needs, is looking for, is willing to compromise on, plus many other matters. The most important thing to keep in mind when preparing to use any of these expressions is that the words you use don't intimidate, undermine, criticize, offend, or cause the other party any discomfort or anger that, in turn, makes them defensive.

# Setting Limits

Setting limits is when someone states he will negotiate only under certain conditions, in a certain location, at a certain time, or in a certain manner. It could also be when a party limits the venue of the negotiation so that they communicate only through their attorney, agent, or some other third party. In history, the French culture has become famous for using time limit in their overall strategy. But it also happens every day in, for example, the food service industry—when someone introduces restrictions on the menu, that's a form of limits!

This technique can really challenge the power dynamics of a negotiation. And it can be done verbally or nonverbally. You might be wondering how the latter works. A nonverbal type of setting limits, known as a "silent barter," is conducted by some tribes in Central Africa. They are engaged in a unique method of negotiating.

Whenever a tribe desires to exchange its goods with those of another tribe, the first group leaves the goods on the bank of a river. The other tribe is expected to take the goods and leave their own goods, considered of equal value, in order to end the negotiation. However, if the second party is not satisfied with the goods, then the goods are simply left on the bank. The first tribe must add to their offerings or else the transaction has ended. The fact that the second tribe will walk away if displeased with the final amount of goods left is an example of setting limits.

## Feinting

Feinting is best summed up by a simple phrase: "Look to the right, go to the left." The three elements involved in most negotiations are concealment, disclosure, and diversion. Feinting is the diversion part, and it occurs whenever someone attempts to divert the other party's attention toward some other issue or matter. In many circumstances, you would use feinting at a time when the other party is getting close to the main source or something that is very important or sensitive to you.

Yet feinting can also be used to promote a false impression. Perhaps you want to convince another person that you have greater knowledge or more information on a subject than you actually have. You would distract them away from what you don't know and suggest that you are more knowledgeable in certain areas than you are.

In some negotiations, feinting can be accomplished by a *conscious* "slip of the tongue," especially when used by someone who is acting as an agent or third person in the transaction. That agent could use such expressions as, "I'm not at liberty to . . .", or "I wish I could tell you more, but. . . ." Then he would go on pretending he's actually getting close to revealing something he shouldn't. Such phrases are excellent hooks that grab immediate attention from those who want to get more information and get to the bottom of matters.

## Association

Those who have grown up in large families and are one of the younger members will easily be able to remember how many times their parents negotiated with them using association. This technique is applied effectively when parents present older brothers and sisters as examples of certain types of conduct and behavior. It is a means of getting a younger child to follow in those footsteps. So a parent might say, "Don't you see how well studying has worked out for David? He just got into one of the best colleges in the nation!" Then the younger sibling, wanting to mimic the older one, will work hard to meet those expectations.

In a negotiation, this tactic is used when a party advises you that a group, company, association, or other party whom you know and respect well has previously done business with them. Association is a powerful magnet not only in drawing attention to what is said but also in influencing others. And no other industry understands such power better than the advertising community. They pay millions of dollars to well-known personalities who positively advertise their products. Consumers *associate* the product with the celebrity and believe that if they buy and use the product, they will be as attractive or successful as that celebrity.

## Disassociation

Disassociation is the opposite of association. It is not only used in politics but also in business. It's pretty straightforward: one party tries to belittle, discourage, or ruin another party by linking them with someone or something undesirable.

In some negotiations, a company comes under scrutiny simply because other firms who manufacture the same or a similar product are under investigation. That first company needs immediately to distance itself from those organizations. Disassociation will be the first tactic out of the bag when the negotiation begins. The first party must assure the other side that "we are the good guys."

## Crossroads

Visualize a crossroads—several paths intersect, entwine, or entangle. When someone uses this tactic, he introduces several matters or issues into the discussion for purposes of getting concessions on one and paving the way or gaining ground on another. Using this method, approaching the other party from several directions, actually forces that other side to see a myriad of issues and concentrate on one of them. In order to feel like they are making progress, that other party will tackle one issue and get the negotiation ball rolling. Then they are more vulnerable and open to others you have placed on the table.

## Blanket

When a person uses the blanket technique, he tries to hit the other party with as many issues as possible, believing that some of them will stick and be resolved. The principle theory in blanketing is, if you cover a wide enough area, you're bound to be successful somewhere. It's like using a shotgun and aiming at a large area, instead of using a rifle and aiming at a much smaller target.

Jerry likes to use the example of a young man who would always select a seat at a movie theatre next to a beautiful woman. In the event you are wondering how he did it in a darkened theatre, the man would choose his seat while the lights were on, before the movie started. As soon as it was dark, he would lean towards the woman and ask for a kiss. There were many times when he received a slap on the face, and many other times the lady would simply get up and select another seat. However, there were also those times when he found someone who was in an equally romantic and daring mood. During those rare finds, the guy was successful at getting a kiss from a pretty girl.

## Randomizing

Randomizing involves picking a sample and assuming that it represents the whole. This is the negotiating method used by someone who is trying to sell a food product in a supermarket or on the sidewalk. The seller offers something to eat for free to those who are passing by. Then, after tasting it, the prospective buyer may be motivated to buy a bagful. However, the sample might have been a particularly sweet or fresh batch. When the consumer gets home and tastes the bagged product, he might find that it is not as good as the morsel he was given by the seller.

There are some negotiations in which the party who is selling products actually brings merchandise, films, or other material for the purpose of convincing the buyer of the quality and performance of his product. The "random" sampling of merchandise will present well. It is an age-old method of closing a deal in business negotiations by letting the other party use the product free of charge.

## Bracketing

The term *bracketing* is actually an old artillery term referring to when a shell is fired in order to register the guns in an artillery battalion. Since Hank was in combat during the Korean War and his responsibility was in "Fire Direction," he knows a great deal about this technique. It is extremely valuable when negotiating because it not only establishes the upper and lower ranges you are dealing with but also the specific areas at which to "aim your guns."

Bracketing directs you toward where it is best to concentrate. It shows you where the majority of troops and equipment are located, so to speak. In other words, it isolates where your best chances for negotiations are.

## Salami

By taking one slice at a time, you can end up with the whole salami. That's the philosophy behind this next approach. The salami technique works exceptionally well in negotiations that involve multiple elements of cost, such as with cases concerning construction. You negotiate not only the overall cost of the project, but such things as design, materials, labor, subcontracts, and more. When Hank was negotiating major weapons contracts with subcontractors in the aerospace industry, this was a major tactic used. Little by little, you gather your information and form a deal.

# Quick Close

The quick close is sometimes saved for when a stalemate must be managed. It is applicable to a situation that seems to be going nowhere, when something has to be done quickly. The quick close occurs when compromising measures are necessary, and so a negotiator will say, "Let's split the difference and get this contract signed," or, "We're willing to meet you halfway."

During our seminars, we have asked attendees if this tactic had worked well for them. The overwhelming response from them has been positive. They claim this tactic remains part of their negotiating techniques. Usually, by the time the quick close is used, both parties are ready to resolve issues; neither is threatening to walk away. And there is usually an urgency involved because of time or financial constraints.

# The Agent of Limited Authority

We will close this long list of effective negotiating techniques with a tactic that allows you to send someone else into the fray. It's for a situation in which you might wish to use an agent rather than to handle it personally because that agent can play the old "I'm not at liberty to make that concession" approach. Thus, he is called the agent of limited authority. If you are a senior member of the negotiating team, the company, the firm, or whatever applies, you probably cannot claim to have your hands tied in too many knots. But an agent of lesser authority cannot be pinned down to anything much because he is locked into an agent-principal relationship and understandably required to respect that relationship.

During negotiations, the agent will make it clear that he is unable to make a firm or final decision without acceptance by the principal. Meanwhile, you can gather a great amount of information concerning what the other party is looking for. This technique also buys you time to really think about what is being proposed. These benefits will greatly assist you when the time comes to make a final decision or judgment.

We have covered nineteen different techniques that are commonly used in negotiations. Believe it or not, there are numerous others—too many to cover all of them here. The ones discussed above are intended to generate some new possibilities in your negotiation repertoire. But always remember to choose strategies that work well with your particular personality and presentation style. You do not want to use a strategy that will appear awkward or disingenuous.

## OVERCOMING AN IMPASSE

Football coach Knute Rockne has been quoted time and time again: "When the going gets tough; the tough get going!" No truer words can be applied when negotiations come to a screeching halt at the table. Everyone who negotiates has, at one time or another, encountered an impasse—that is, a time when both sides seem to be at a standstill and the negotiation is going nowhere. At one of our seminars, an attendee interrupted us when we began discussing this topic and blurted out, "You mean a deadlock?" And our response was, "Some people call it that, but we think that word sounds too fatal, insurmountable."

Negotiators tend to return to the familiar when faced with an impasse; they rely on anywhere from three to six different methods or tactics that have worked for them in previous negotiations. And they hope beyond hope that one of those approaches will work once again. However, what happens when that handful of techniques proves ineffective? Negotiators can't "punt the ball" as a desperate football team can. Instead, we have to continue to handle the ball.

The best way to prepare yourself for an impasse is to have knowledge of more than three or four resolving tactics. Gather as many approaches as you can, so that you won't be at a loss when the "old faithful" don't work. When we originally covered this subject in our seminars, we used to discuss approximately six to nine different methods of breaking an impasse. Then we would open up the program to all the attendees and invite them to share with us any other suggestions. As a result, we enlarged our list to eighteen methods of how to deal with an impasse, all of which are covered in this section.

When you have completed reading them, perhaps you can add a few more to the list.

## Take a Break

Take a break or caucus for a few minutes—or longer. If you are part of a team, use the time to discuss matters and brainstorm with the other team members. If you are working alone, get up from the table and walk around the room, look out the window, or simply go to the water fountain or the bathroom down the hall. Such periods of reassessment can often generate new ideas and fresh insights.

We believe it is very important during your recess not to talk about throwing in the towel and walking away. Always save that as the very last resort and action. Such negative thinking has a habit of becoming contagious and can destroy productive and creative thinking.

## Recap What Has Occurred

Together, both your party and the other party should review and discuss what has been agreed upon so far, or what exactly is causing disagreement. Also, discuss the agreements-in-principle that were reached over the course of the negotiation thus far, as well as common interests. Sometimes you will discover that the results you have mutually achieved are more significant than perhaps realized. This will spark you on to further resolution. And whenever you talk about something positive, it reflects that the time spent has not been wasted.

## Decide What Will Be Lost

Mutually, clearly find the answer to the question, "What will be lost if we call it quits at this point?" There are times during an impasse when both sides temporarily forget the negative side of not reaching a settlement. Terminating the negotiation is an outcome that will be detrimental to all concerned. This is a time when it is important to discuss the "minuses" of not resolving the issues.

Hank recalls a negotiation in which he described a possible negative outcome if the two sides were not to reach a settlement. The visualization of failure that he provided actually triggered new resolve in the other party. Someone interrupted him and stated, "Your crystal ball is cloudy. And I'll clear it up for you." And then that person proceeded to speak in a much more positive manner. The tide was turned and negotiations continued. Thus we have discovered that, in some instances, when a person creates a negative image, another individual often tries to make it look less detrimental. Perhaps this occurs because most of us carry around a positive self-image. And whenever it is challenged, we psychologically rise to the occasion to make it less negative. We're not suggesting you harp on the dark side of matters throughout your negotiations, but at certain times, a little talk of the "doom" that might follow if the impasse continues can actually inspire a break in the impasse.

## Express How You Feel

When you communicate your feelings, you present yourself as very relatable. Others will acknowledge that you have let your guard down and then possibly do the same. This tactic may uncover and reveal that the other side feels exactly the same way. Even if you haven't reached agreement on any issue, at least you can admit that you have similar emotions.

Once you have honestly expressed how frustrated you feel about the impasse and hopefully heard the return frustration from the other party, take a deep breath and say, "Since it appears that we both feel the same way, let's do something about it!" Make the statement nonverbally convincing by moving your upper body forward and rubbing your palms together in a gesture of expectation. You will appear to be a team player for both sides, amiable and optimistic.

## Change the Subject

Although this sounds like you are throwing a red herring into the mix, introduce another issue, view, or approach. Don't belabor the subject that has gotten both of you tied up in knots. Whenever you do this, you're not sweeping the topic under the table; you're simply setting it aside for a while. If the other side refuses to change subjects, explain that moving to other issues does not mean you are forgetting the unresolved ones. Instead, you believe that the "cooling" effect of switching to other matters can be very effective.

## Attempt to Secure an Agreement-in-Principle

The topic of agreements-in-principle was discussed in Chapter 4 (see page 95). There, we defined agreements-in-principle as mutual goals to which the parties commit themselves, such as the agreement not to walk away without some sort of resolution, or not to drag the negotiations on beyond two weeks. There are some agreements-in-principle that are rather simple to get because they formulate the fundamental reason why the two sides are negotiating. They may be stated as, "We agree we have to work out some kind of compromise in order to . . .", or "We're both here to negotiate whatever differences exist . . .", and also, "We both are aware we need each other, therefore we have to. . . ." Such statements pave the way for getting agreements-in-principle, regardless of how flimsy they may be.

Needs are the cornerstones of why we negotiate. Sometimes parties' needs differ, and sometimes they don't. But usually you can find something in common with the other side. Always rely on those needs that you both have. In the long run, finding common ground won't let you down.

## Try Bridge-Issue Agreements

In many negotiations there are innocuous issues that are of little importance and can be easily agreed to. These rather benign issues are also sometimes used in breaking a situation that is deadlocked. No one understands this better than a marriage counselor acting as a third party in negotiating differences in a troubled marriage. Such a counselor would work on establishing common basic agreements from the couple on relatively minor issues in their union. Once he has accomplished that, he will then move on to tacking other, more sensitive issues.

A good example can be found in a labor dispute in which the union demands were as follows: (1) a 17 percent increase in pay; (2) greater retirement benefits; (3) more voice in management decisions that affect workers; (4) changes in the grievance procedures; and (5) changes in the color (black) of the uniforms worn by employees because it was too depressing. In this negotiation, it would be wise for management to use the last demand as the bridge-issue. Once establishing an agreement on it, a more relaxed and less defensive attitude might exist in discussing and negotiating the other issues.

## Discuss What Alternatives Remain

The effect of redirecting the discussion from an impasse to what alternatives remain may switch the negotiation from a negative to a positive course. And if the response is that there are no other alternatives, don't let it bother you. Get creative! In a buy-sell situation in which you are the seller, discouragement makes it very easy for the buyer to say goodbye. Developing creative alternatives is what separates the successful negotiator from those with much lower batting averages. We have a colleague who loves telling others in such situations, "There are always other alternatives. We just haven't found them yet!" And he uses emphasis on the word "yet."

## Make an Important Disclosure

In most negotiations, each party knows something the other one doesn't know. And some of this knowledge is more important than the rest. Therefore, in some sense, negotiating is a process of, "What do you know that I don't know?" Whenever important disclosures are made, they are usually received with enthusiasm.

In an impasse, disclosing something of importance that will benefit the other party is like a peace offering. It usually breaks through the bottleneck. But a word of caution is necessary: should you disclose something of major importance, always do it incrementally, instead of blurting it out all at once. Make the other party work to get the information, don't merely "spill your guts." The more they work at squeezing all the information out of you, the more they will have a tendency to believe it is the truth, and nothing but the truth. You will also, therefore, have opened up the doors of communication, convincing them that if they keep working at this negotiation, their time and efforts will be worth it.

## Ask a Hypothetical Question

Asking a "what if" question may be very effective when used at the appropriate moment in your negotiation. And if you choose to do this, don't allow the words you use to get you into hot water by saying something that may possibly be misinterpreted. During your preparation, give some thought as to how hypothetical questions should be worded in order not to be misunderstood. We have seen instances in which the words were carelessly spoken and the listener heard something that was different. Remember again, the message is always in the receiver's ear, not in the sender's mouth. But an effective hypothetical question can extend the range of vision, helping the negotiators to see the bigger picture and work for resolution.

## Ask for or Offer Empathy

When negotiating, we've all heard expressions like, "I know exactly how you feel," "I've been in your shoes," or "I see your position, but. . . ." There are times when showing empathy towards others is beneficial. When your hands are tied by individuals or conditions, words of empathy are truly heartening. When others can understand the limits that have been imposed on you, they are more likely to be empathic. So don't be afraid to ask for such understanding. Perhaps you could say, "If I could ask you to step into my shoes for a moment and see things from my position, together we might be able to find another way to handle this situation." Asking for empathy is especially effective in a situation in which you are acting as an agent for a principle and unable to make a total settlement without your principle's concurrence.

It is also important to remember to offer empathy once in a while. It is possible that when you display empathetic responses towards others, some individuals will take it as sign of weakness and attempt to squeeze you in order to get as much as they can. If they try, you should certainly pull back and explain that your intention was to be responsibly open-minded, not taken advantage of. But the other party might also appreciate your willingness to see things their way. Emphasize the fact that you are trying to see the situation from all angles. They might very much respect your fairness and respond to you in a like manner. Don't forget that the negotiating process is giving and getting, getting and giving, hopefully in equal measure!

## Try Using a Quick Close

In some negotiations, the impasse has occurred for a very simple reason. One or both sides have been jockeying for position and the negotiation has reached a point at which the players intuitively sense a "quick close" offer may work. This approach has already been defined as a negotiation technique on page 113. However, it is worth mentioning as a possible route to break an impasse as well. When a "quick close" is timed correctly, a phrase such as, "Will you take $49,000 for it, and that way we can finish today?" or, "What do you say we settle this at $25,400 and both get back to work", can bring closure to a trying negotiation.

As so often occurs in life, three things are likely to happen. First, the other party may readily accept the close and then shake your hand, cementing the deal. Second, they may reject the offer and call it quits. Third, they might counter with another figure. Regardless of what happens, the impasse has been broken.

## Diagram Differences

A seminar attendee once told us that she disliked negotiating at locations that didn't have a blackboard or a flipchart in the room. And the main reason for this was because she felt using visual aids for purposes of illustrating differences was extremely important in breaking deadlock and differences. She firmly believed that visualization is a key to opening up closed doors when communicating with others. So she would literally make a list of the points of disagreement, and then work through them.

And we agree with her. When something is illustrated, the narrowness of differences between two parties becomes apparent. As that old expression states, "Seeing is believing!" Whenever narrow differences are seen instead of heard, it seems to have a completely different compromising effect on people.

## Give Something to Get Something

A surefire tactic that will overcome an impasse is making a compromise offer. Perhaps one of the most frequently asked questions by workshop attendees is, "When do I make a compromise?" That question may be answered by looking at the many different reasons for making compromises. And the reason we put in last place is that you feel compelled or forced to do it. That brings to mind the words of Winston Churchill when describing an appeaser: "Someone who feeds a crocodile, hoping it will eat him last!"

The word *compromise* culturally seems to convey a more negative than positive image. Perhaps most of us grow up with this negative conception because when we were young, an adult told us, "Never compromise!" Apparently they didn't have the wisdom to realize that life is a long process of negotiating with others, and in order to satisfy our own and others' needs, we must compromise! The *art of negotiating* consists of knowing how, why, where, to whom, and when to make concessions.

## Bring Up Future Needs

In most negotiations, present needs are the most important and critical in discussions, despite the fact that the same needs often existed yesterday, and will tomorrow. All of our needs fall into one or all three of those categories. However, during negotiations, present needs always seem to take center stage. Have you ever considered trying the approach of pointing out how you can help the *future* of the other party if they work on a deal with you now?

In some negotiations, individuals are truly unaware of future needs they may have unless you open their eyes and mind to them. Most of us are locked into what needs are pulling at us today, but tomorrow's needs are equally important. Breaking an impasse by bringing up the possibility that you'll be in position to satisfy their future needs, if required, is a great bargaining chip.

## Discuss Good Association

An impasse may sometimes be handled by talking about all the favorable and productive dealings the two sides have shared. Bring up all of those "remember when's." Can you retrieve a desperate and difficult time you both faced that was overcome by your mutual cooperative efforts? Every personal or business relationship you have in life is full of such experiences. And turning to that page of the scrapbook, so to speak, can and may be used effectively during times of stress, conflict, or other difficulties. It's the "we've gotten through this before" approach.

Also, it is worthwhile remembering that trust and goodwill are not mere words to negotiators. They are the backbone and cornerstone of the negotiating process. Therefore, when facing an impasse, returning to them and reflecting on past periods of trust and goodwill may bridge present differences.

## Change Locations

In some instances, simply changing locations might help overcome the impasse and save your negotiation. Getting out of the conference room or office and walking to the manufacturing area, touring the accounting department, or looking at engineering drawings may influence attitudes. Even simply standing up by the coffee machine may do it. Consider the fact that negotiations conducted while standing up don't last as long as those when seated!

## Call It Quits

We have saved this alternative for last simply because it should only be employed as the last resort. It doesn't take much creativity to stand up and leave when things aren't going well for you. And if you choose to do it, remember you may have to "eat crow" at a later time.

Walking out may require you to come back and later apologize or ask forgiveness. So unless you're sure your departure will jolt the other party and change their attitude concerning making a compromise, it's probably in your best interest not to do it.

There is no other time during a negotiation when you must become more creative than when the process has reached a stalemate—when it's going nowhere, when both sides are deadlocked. That's usually the point when you believe you have two options, which are to "punt the ball" or to "run like hell" for the nearest exit. Yet that's also a time for realizing that you have a great number of creative alternatives for purposes of breaking the impasse and continuing to earnestly negotiate. We hope that our suggestions have inspired you to keep trying and to venture outside of your comfort zone if the old familiar tactics just aren't making headway for you.

## CONDUCTING LATERAL THINKING

We're not done with creative techniques yet. There is another avenue of creativity well worth discussing, and it is called lateral thinking. The term was coined by Edward de Bono, who has written several books on the subject in Great Britain. Lateral thinking refers to taking a different approach in solving problems, seeking to find new insights and alternative methods of resolution. It is a creative process every negotiator should be aware of and beneficially use.

Lateral thinking requires focusing on a problem or situation from a totally different perspective or point of view. And when you do so, you may make what appears to be a very difficult situation quite simple to handle. For example, an executive who worked for a utility and power company in Omaha, Nebraska, told us story of how his sixteen-year-old daughter once saved the city from a total collapse of power before a second ice storm was due to hit the city.

During breakfast, the executive told his family to prepare for a loss of power because the ice storm that had hit the city a day before had deposited a considerable amount of ice on the power lines. Another storm was on its way that would add to the ice, causing the power lines to collapse under the weight. He told them his company didn't have enough equipment or manpower to remove the ice that had already been deposited on the power lines. His daughter laughed at what he had told them and remarked, "Dad, that's no problem. I know how you can remove all the ice very quickly." The man looked at his daughter and asked, "What do you mean?" The daughter quickly answered, "It's simple, just get a couple of helicopters and have them fly low over the power lines. The vibration they create will knock all the ice off the lines in a jiffy!"

Lateral thinking is closely related to creativity, but whereas creativity is often the description of a result, lateral thinking is a description of a process. Humor is lateral thinking; that's the reason why people laugh at the unexpected punch line. Winston Churchill was a great lateral thinker and had a great sense of humor as a result. Two stories often repeated about him in Great Britain clearly illustrate this.

Lady Astor was an aristocrat who disliked Churchill very much. On one occasion, while both were attending a social function, Lady Astor remarked to Churchill, "Sir Winston, if I was your wife I would put poison in your tea!" Churchill immediately retorted, "Lady Astor, if I were your husband I would drink it!"

The other story concerns a time when Churchill was falling asleep in the House of Commons with the fly of his trousers wide open. Another member rudely said, "Sir Winston, you're disgusting! Just look at the open fly of your trousers!" Churchill gave him a faint smile and answered, "Not to worry; sleeping birds seldom fall out of their nests!"

When things become too serious and tempers flare up in a negotiation, there are times when a person can put the negotiation back on track by telling a creative joke. It temporarily loosens up all of the negotiators, and it makes use of lateral thinking. But lateral thinking certainly does not have to be humorous. The process simply involves thinking outside the box, or taking a look at things from a totally different angle.

We have also discovered that sometimes it is also worthwhile, for creative purposes, to twist someone's words around and restate them a different word order. In some instances this has sparked creative thoughts, because individuals then see things in a different manner.

A classic example of lateral thinking—seeing, not looking, at something in a different light—was the medical discovery of how the human kidney functions. For years physiologists were unable to understand the purpose of the long loops in the kidney tubules. So it had been assumed that the loops had no special function and were a relic of the way in which the kidney had evolved in humans. And then one day an engineer looked at the loops and at once recognized that they could be part of a counter-current multiplier—a well-known engineering device for increasing the concentration of solutions. In that instant, a fresh new look from outside had provided an answer to something that had been a puzzle for a very long time. The practice of seeing from a different vantage point, or through the eyes of someone who has a different background or training, can be very worthwhile and valuable.

In order to become more aware during the course of a negotiation, and thereby more creative, it is necessary to shift from the obvious way of looking at things to a less obvious one. In other words, don't solely concentrate on what is happening; also be aware of what is *not* happening. A shift of view brings out creativity. That was how a cure for smallpox occurred, when Edward Jenner shifted his attention from why people get smallpox to why dairy maids apparently did not. From this switch of attention, he discovered that harmless cowpox gave the dairy maids protection against deadly smallpox. Jenner's discovery subsequently lead to the development of a vaccine for preventing smallpox. Impressive, isn't it?

The fundamental reason many of us are not adept at lateral thinking is simply because of our educational experience. The learning methods we were exposed to were geared toward logic, and so we learned to solve problems using the left side of the brain. Personally, we don't recall any teacher ever stating, "Sometimes it helps to solve a problem by rearranging order, structure, and relationship." Do you? But that doesn't mean you can't start thinking laterally today. Try it. The more freedom you give yourself, the more creative you'll become in your negotiating demands, resolutions, and reputation.

# AVOIDING THE PITFALL OF HIDDEN ASSUMPTIONS

As we near the end of this chapter on effective things to do in the negotiation process, we have to include a discussion of something *not* to do. Most people rely on assumptions when trying to make a decision, resolve an issue, or argue a point. The problem is that the majority of people never examine their assumptions, let alone test them to see if they are worth maintaining. Whoever first wrote or said, "When we assume, we make an 'ass' out of 'u' and 'me,'" was a very wise person. Interestingly, there are very few additional quotations that have been written on the word *assume* and its effect on our lives. Dictionaries hold multiple definitions for the word, but the one that most directly pertains to negotiating involves the idea that when we assume something, we take it for granted that a projected circumstance is true or that a projected outcome will occur.

For a long time, we thought that the words *assume* and *believe* were very similar and should be synonyms. Yet when used in conversation, the word *assume* seems weaker in conviction than the word *believe;* the latter seems to have a much stronger basis than the former. Starting from a very early age, we begin to make assumptions and develop beliefs; it is a process that continues throughout life. In fact, we must accept that assuming and believing are part of human nature. And human nature is definitely present at the negotiating table. Therefore, since we're going to continue making assumptions, there are two things we can do. The first is to become aware that we're making them. And the second thing is to test them, to see if they are true or false. Let's learn just how to do that.

# A More Thorough Definition of Assumptions

Some assumptions are relatively simple. For example, we hand a store clerk our money and expect her to give us our merchandise and sometimes also change in return. Whenever we mail a check along with a subscription to a magazine, we expect to subsequently receive that publication. And a traveler who boards an airliner destined for Chicago assumes it will land at O'Hare Airport—or at a more convenient airport in the event of any emergency.

But assumptions brought to negotiations are different. Every assumption made before, during, or after a negotiation may turn out to be a serious mental error that will later keep us awake at night. Furthermore, all of our assumptions are fundamentally based on perception. And to make matters worse, humans don't see everything they look at. "Looking" is two-dimensional, while "seeing" is three-dimensional.

During our seminars on negotiating we used to prove this point very easily by asking the attendees how many of them had ever seen a rainbow. Usually, all or most of them would raise their hands. And then we would ask who, of those who had seen a rainbow before, was absolutely sure of how many colors they perceived (saw). After this question, the number of raised hands considerably lessened. Of those whose hands still remained raised, approximately only one-half answered accurately, stating they saw five colors. Finally, we asked how many knew the exact color sequence of a rainbow, from the inside out. In all the years we asked this question, we never had a single attendee give us the correct color sequence. Then we would drive our point home on the difference between "looking" and "seeing." We would inform them, "You have looked at a rainbow, but you have never actually seen one. If you had, you would have observed that the color sequence is violet, blue, orange, yellow, and red." (By the way, if you want to remember this little bit of trivia, think of the letter "V," followed by the word "boy," and then the letter "R".)

Alfred Adler, in his great book *Understanding Human Nature*, wrote, "The majority of mankind is probably visual-minded. They fill in the mosaic picture of the world which they have created for themselves. These perceptions need not be strictly identical with actuality. Everyone is capable of reconfiguring and rearranging their contacts with the outer world to fit their life pattern." And so it is when we sit down to negotiate with others; we have developed our own pictures beforehand and often try desperately to make the other party fit our perceptions—our assumptions—including all the baggage we believe that party carries.

There are times when making an assumption and later finding out that it was false causes no harm because it wasn't serious. However, there are also times in life when the consequences are very grave. In the medical profession, a doctor's worse nightmare is if his "anchor" judgment is wrong. The medical term *anchor* refers to a quick, snap diagnosis the doctor makes the first time he examines you. Based on his initial assumption, he will then pursue testing and/or treat you accordingly.

As negotiators, we are not in life-or-death types of situations like medical doctors are. Yet the false assumptions we make and perpetuate can and do eventually lead to serious consequences. It is true that assumptions are a valid and important part of negotiations. But we must be extra careful not to make them unnecessarily. Unfortunately, there are many who don't realize a large part of our beliefs are based on unconscious, hidden assumptions that are biased.

Hidden assumptions are very difficult to bring into the open and recognize. They are like icebergs, nine-tenths submerged (unconscious), with only a small portion above the water (conscious). Assumption-making isn't taught or learned in the same manner that we learn mathematics or spelling, for example, during our educational process. We simply process bits and pieces of information that we pick up from our senses, and we automatically use past experiences and patterns when we make assumptions. Moreover, we believe assumptions are, to a great extent, heavily influenced by what we perceive nonverbally.

Hidden assumptions are not subject to rational verification, as other assumptions might be. If we make an open assumption that a certain chair will support our weight and it does, then our assumption was correct. If it doesn't, we take a "pratfall" and land on our behind. In such a case, we get an immediate verification that our assumption was either right or wrong. And if wrong, it is easy to laugh off—no big deal, just select another, stronger chair to sit on. There is absolutely nothing wrong with making the assumption that most chairs will hold your weight. But a problem does arise when we think and behave as if an assumption that judges people is absolutely a proven fact.

In our seminars we deal with assumptions. We hold up a pencil and ask the attendees to describe and write down what they see. Everyone thinks it's a normal pencil they're seeing. However, they are surprised when we bend the pencil and they see it's an artificial rubber pencil bought at a novelty store.

What's the point in discussing hidden assumptions? Well, if we become sensitive to the fact that we all make assumptions and act accordingly, we can be prepared for the unexpected and are less likely to dogmatically defend our positions if we are proven to be wrong. Following are two such examples.

A Catholic priest is taking his morning walk and sees an unshaved, raggedly dressed man leaning against the side of a building. The priest makes the assumption that the bedraggled man is homeless. He approaches the man, gives him a ten-dollar bill, and counsels, "Never despair!" Then the priest walks away. The following morning the priest sees the same man at the same spot, and he is surprised when the man beckons the priest to come close to him. When the priest is very close, the man looks around to see if anyone is looking at them, and then hands the priest a small white envelope while saying, "Never Despair won and paid ten to one!" What the priest perceived to be a homeless man turned out to be a bookie.

The other example occurs when you're at party with friends, and someone tells you that they just saw a beggar walk out of the ladies room. What is your first assumption? It probably was that the beggar was a man. Was it?

## Evaluations of Assumptions

The assumptions we make are a vital part of our human communication system. We use them continuously in sorting out and trying to make sense of the millions of ambiguous mental stimuli that confront us. We receive a communication, quickly interpret it, and make a first guess—an assumption that which we stay with until it is disproved. As the Gestalt school of psychology puts it, to probe a hole we first use a stick to see how far it takes us. We might paraphrase this and say that, to understand the world by probing, we use assumptions until they are disproved. It must be remembered that simple assumptions are easy to refute. However, hidden ones are very difficult to recognize and refute or correct.

Yet during a negotiation there are ways of testing the assumptions you've made. One of them is by asking questions. For example, you've made the assumption that the person with whom you're negotiating has the authority to settle and make a deal with you. All the inductive and deductive information you've received and perceived, verbally and nonverbally, indicates this. But, early in the discussion, you should ask: "In the event you find our terms and conditions acceptable, are you willing to sign the contract today so we can get started on your project?" This question will normally receive one of three responses: "Yes," "No," or "It all depends." Then he will give you additional information that tells you if the assumption is correct or not.

Another method of testing assumptions you've made is by using hypothetical situations. For example, imagine that you are negotiating with a firm that may be protected by some recently legislated environmental laws. In your negotiation, you're dealing with several issues that require knowledge concerning prospective problems—the type of issues your corporate attorneys believe will require escape clauses. You have assumed that any subsequent changes calling for your company's implementation will be separately negotiated. Furthermore, you have assumed that your firm will be reimbursed for any such expenses incurred, which are over and above what you are presently negotiating. You can then test your assumption by creating a hypothetical situation in which a worse case scenario becomes a reality. And then you ask questions relative to who will be responsible for the expenses. In this scenario, you will not only discuss any changes, but also, how soon you will know about them, and how long it will take to implement them.

Sometimes you can also use the old standby, "What if. . . ." It is especially useful in negotiating construction contracts that may later be affected by federal, state, or local building codes. In many instances, the firm responsible for the construction *assumes* that any such incurred changes will be borne by the customer or buyer. You need to know how such a situation would be managed. So ask, "What if electrical codes change and the building has to be retrofitted?" During the course of a negotiation, you seldom are privy to seeing the "boiler plate" clauses in a prospective customer's contracts. Even if you have many years of experience, don't assume that you know exactly what the small print on a document covers.

And a final method of testing assumptions is accomplished by listening carefully to what is said, what is implied, and most important, what is not said. This requires full-time attention throughout the negotiation, not simply at the beginning as so many negotiators think. For this reason, we strongly recommend that in a team-type negotiation, one person be assigned the specific task of being the listener. And don't give the assignment to the person who will be the scribe. If you do, you will regret it because an individual cannot take adequate notes and listen carefully at the same time. The scribe records what is said, while the listener hears things between the lines.

## Acknowledgement That Assumptions Can Also Work in Your Favor

Of course, making assumptions is not always disastrous. Actually, there are times when the ability to correctly anticipate the other party's assumptions may lead to successful results in business. We would be remiss if we did not acknowledge that before ending this section on assumptions. There are not many individuals who try to circumvent the government legally by anticipating its assumptions and thus making their own. Many hope of one day finding a legal loop-hole in the regulations that they can squeeze through. Some who found such a loop-hole have become legends to others who tried and failed.

For many years, the U.S. Customs Authority made it almost impossible to get around the rigid customs regulations they established. However, one clever importer found an opening and did it. She accomplished it by carefully studying the regulations, and by anticipating certain assumptions that the customs people would make and try to enforce. She discovered that French leather gloves made for women carried a high import duty, which made them very expensive in the United States. So she took a trip to France and bought ten-thousand pairs of the most expensive ladies gloves she was able to find. She then came up with a very creative idea of separating all the pairs of gloves and made a shipment of ten thousand left-hand gloves to the United States.

And when the shipment was made, she didn't claim it. Instead, she allowed it to stay in customs until the period for claiming it had expired. When this occurs, according to regulations, customs has to put an unclaimed shipment up for auction. They did so.

Now, can you possibly imagine anyone who would be foolish enough to buy a shipment of ten-thousand left-hand ladies gloves? Well, there was one bidder—an agent working for the importer— who bought them for a very small amount of money.

Meanwhile, the customs authorities smelled something fishy and alerted their employees to be on the alert for a similar shipment of right-hand ladies gloves. They were determined not to allow the importer to get away with her scheme. But the creative importer had anticipated such action and the assumption that the shipment would once again be made in the same manner: one shipment of ten thousand right-hand ladies gloves. So she cleverly packaged the right-hand gloves in two per box. The importer wisely "assumed" that a department official checking the shipment would also "assume" that each box contained one for the right hand and one for the left and allow the shipment to pass through customs. Her gamble worked perfectly. It passed through and she paid duty only on five-thousand pairs, plus a very small amount for those she had claimed at auction.

We compliment a negotiator who is capable of correctly sorting out what "preconceived assumptions" the other party has made, and who is able not only to isolate them but also to plan a means of taking advantage of them. That is a very creative and capable negotiator. He is someone you would dearly love to have on your side and not on the other side of the table.

## The Importance of an Open Mind

Tom Lantos, a beloved congressman from California, died in early 2008 at the age of eighty. During his productive life, he often used a saying of great significance: "The mind is a parachute. The only time it works is when it's open!" He was born in Hungary and spent several years in a concentration camp during World War II. He was the only member of the U.S. Congress who had that experience.

The experiences we absorb over many years influence and shape our judgments and the decisions we make, thus creating prejudices and bias. It is very important to realize that particular experiences don't have the same meaning and impact on others, who have formed and developed their own assumptions. When negotiating in different cultures, such differences are magnified. In such cases, in order to be responsible human beings, we must take into consideration both our inner assumptions and those of the other people involved.

A seminar attendee once offered some great wisdom concerning this difference. He stated that at the beginning of a negotiation he had done something that had worked extremely well. It was based on his belief that conflict is often the result of misunderstandings and false assumptions. As soon as the hand-shaking and introductions were concluded and before any statements of issues were uttered, he would say something similar to the following: "Although we both approach this negotiation with preconceived ideas, views, and assumptions, my sincere hope is that we mutually don't forget to keep an open mind to whatever is said." By not ending his comment with a question, he cleverly did not ask for a response. This man told us that in the majority of his negotiations, the other party usually stated they had a similar attitude and feeling. When the attendee had finished sharing his experience with us, we quickly alerted him that he had given us a wonderful example of successfully using an "agreement-in-principle." (See page 95.)

The reason we assume is that we have absorbed an incredible number of impressions during our lives from which we mentally form judgments. But we need to understand that each individual has his own private inner world. As a result of this, judging what is right or wrong is highly biased. So when it comes to making assumptions and judgments about the other negotiator or the other party, do your best to keep an open mind.

Hidden assumptions may negatively influence your objective thinking and decisions when you are unaware that they exist. They are capable of completely misleading you in what you hear and see. During negotiations, we sometimes place ourselves at a great disadvantage because of our hidden assumptions concerning other people's motivations, interests, and actions. While it is impossible to engage in a negotiation without hidden assumptions, it is possible to be aware of them and test them for accuracy. Doing so will greatly benefit your judgment and the decisions you will make.

## CONCLUSION

We have covered everything from pondering power dynamics to selecting strategies and tactics, from breaking impasses to testing assumptions. Along the way, we have even suggested a technique for thinking—lateral thinking! Essentially, this chapter has prepared you to enter your next negotiation in a confident, creative, and unbiased manner. By now, you understand quite well how to conduct your agenda, manage your relationship with the other party, and make the most of the art of negotiating. But there's still more to think about. Chapter 6 will venture into a more profound discussion on your team.

# 6

# Different Perspectives, Same Goals

## The Manager and the Team

*"Your ability to negotiate, communicate, influence, and persuade others to do things is absolutely indispensable to everything you accomplish in life. The most effective men and women in every area are those who can quite competently organize the cooperation and assistance of other people toward the accomplishment of important goals and objectives."*

—BRIAN TRACY

We have discovered something that many executives and managers are not aware of, despite the fact that it occurs on a daily basis. Moreover, it is something that is extremely important to their success in management. What is it? Managers and others in similar positions of authority tend to be better at negotiating skills when it comes to external affairs than when they must negotiate internally. This was discovered in a very unusual, unexpected manner. It was during an in-house seminar for managers that Hank conducted for a major corporation.

At the beginning of the program, Hank requested, "Please take a few moments and write down on a piece of paper what word, in your opinion, best describes your management function and/or responsibility." Afterwards, he collected all the papers from the participants and read aloud the words they had written. Common answers included the following terms: manage; direct; control; authorize; lead; delegate; supervise; evaluate; promote; hire; and fire. Only *one* person had written the word *negotiate.*

During the daily course of business, every supervisor, manager, and executive has to negotiate constantly with many individuals in order to fulfill her respective management responsibilities. And yet most are unaware of how often they do so. The dictionary defines *management* as an art, but one that is characterized by control and the giving of directions. Interestingly, most dictionaries do not give a synonym for "manager" or "management." Yet we can so easily replace that word with "chief negotiator." Why do managers or executives not see themselves as negotiators within their own companies? Why do they generally tend not to see the importance of being great internal negotiators? Let's explore this issue.

## The Effects of Ego

A major oil company asked us to conduct a series of seminars for their executives on the subject of effective negotiating in management. This occurred because one of their executives had attended our public seminar on negotiating and wanted an answer to a question that had been bothering him for a long time. He wanted to understand why so many of his company's personnel did such a great job of negotiating situations with outside sources, and yet were considerably less effective when it came to negotiating internally with the firm's own supervisors, managers, and executives. Great question!

It took a period of three years to process all of that company's managers and executives through our program, and we learned a great deal about the dynamics of organizational management and negotiating. We also found that after experiencing the two-day seminars, most attendees were amazed at what little awareness they previously had of how much internal negotiating was required in order to satisfactorily fulfill their management duties. For some reason, they considered the art of negotiating to be something they did with another party, not their own. We also discovered that individuals in marketing and sales—who tend to spend a great amount of their time negotiating with individuals outside of their firm—were more effective negotiators in general than those who primarily negotiated within the organization, with other employees.

A sales manager during one program mentioned that he actually had noticed an emotional difference in the sales staff when negotiating within the company, as opposed to when dealing with customers. He had observed that when individuals negotiated situations and problems internally, they seemed to be more "thin-skinned." They were more sensitive to criticism and tended to react in a more negative manner then when they were dealing with customers. Another executive who was in charge of procurement also mentioned he had observed that purchasing agents for the corporation seemed to be much better at negotiating with suppliers and sub-contract vendors than with having to deal with subordinates or other company employees.

In order to find out specific reasons why there was such a difference in how individuals negotiated internally and externally, we decided to get the answers from the attendees themselves. So during the final two hours of each seminar, we asked the attendees for their own experiences, ideas, and feedback.

There was a consensus that an individual's ego was a contributing factor, and that it was displayed with different intensity during internal and external negotiations. Whenever an agent for a company is involved in an external negotiation, her ego doesn't seem to get in the way of closing a deal, getting an order, or reaching a settlement. In those situations, a person tends to be very good at taking the ego out of the word "nEGOtiating." Her overall behavior is congruent with her objectivity of nailing a deal, so she doesn't allow personal emotions to affect the achieving of results. But when negotiating internally in an organization, the ego is much more evident in how an individual defensively reacts to criticism or other negative comments directed at her.

The seminar attendees with whom we were working also expressed belief that organizational authority, rank, or level was another influential factor. When negotiating externally, a person's authority is important only relative to how much power she has as an agent. This is especially true with regards to commitments, binding agreements, credibility, and the like. Her rank within her own company does not matter much to the other party; she cannot give orders that the other party must comply with and follow. However, in internal matters, authority and rank are very strong factors. Indeed, there are often situations when a person with greater authority refuses to discuss or negotiate a situation and simply demands what she wants. And whomever she has given orders to either follows them or runs the risk of censure or dismissal. Again, this goes back to ego.

## The Importance of a Relaxed Environment

During the discussions with attendees, they also mentioned how important it is to negotiate staff meetings in order to make them not only more effective, but also more productive in generating greater creativity, in solving problems, and in developing new ideas. The first thing the executives mentioned was that it is important to create an informal environment where humor is welcomed and encouraged. The majority of them agreed that many of their meetings started out with a serious and somber environment. It was suggested that perhaps a good idea would be to start every staff meeting with a joke that might set a relaxed mood and make people more comfortable.

When individuals feel comfortable they tend to be more willing to express their feelings without any fear of censure. They make statements that contain a great amount of honesty, including emotional statements. And the more emotionally honest individuals are at staff meetings, the more the group benefits and the greater the members' awareness of the situation, problem, or condition. At organizational staff meetings, many problems that arise for discussion are not simply physical, technical, or economic. Many of them are psychological and have deep emotional sources that need to be revealed and understood. Such problems need to be expressed in order to bring them out for all to become aware of and find solutions for.

# The Encouragement of Honesty and Openness

Another suggestion the executives under discussion came up with was to encourage everyone to be assertive in expressing what they believe, and to discourage any negative, aggressive, or defensive reactions to what someone said. If a manager, for example, felt a defensiveness rising after a staff member critiqued a certain aspect of the department, she should ask questions of that staff member that might reveal additional information that would shed additional light on the present beliefs and feelings. Don't shoot down the concerns; discuss them! And perhaps that might also lead to a solution or answer. When a team pools thoughts together, more solutions tend to rise out of the pile. One senior executive commented that he wished he had been exposed to understanding and learning more about "negotiating staff meetings" when he was younger. If he had, he would not have committed so many errors in the past and his meetings would have been much more fruitful and rewarding.

We have also discovered that staff meetings are much more productive if the person leading them asks questions instead of making statements. For example, if it is a sales meeting, the purpose might be more effectively stated if it is posed as a question: "What can we do to increase our overall sales next quarter?" instead of making a statement such as, "We must increase sales next quarter." A question motivates and stimulates creative thinking and develops new ideas and concepts, whereas strict statements are received as commands and instructions, making individuals resentful and defensive.

What we contribute to the recommendations is the advice not to record a staff meeting on audio or videotape. Whenever it is recorded, individuals tend to be very guarded in what they say. Therefore, they fail to disclose information for fear that it will somehow be used against them later. It is all right to take notes and later transcribe them into a complete report on what transpired during the meeting, and to distribute that report to all who attended. But making the attendees feels as though they are on stage or under scrutiny during the actual meeting will not encourage honest, open discussion.

## The Benefits of Positive and Creative Language

We also suggest to the senior manager who has called a staff meeting that she develop and use positively charged words, such as "immediate action," "visible results," and "effective involvement." Positively charged words not only work very well for athletic coaches to spur athletes to achieve greater performance, but they also do wonders in lifting the spirits and motivation of employees, especially if morale is rather low in an organization.

Hank once worked for a senior executive who did this in a very unusual and creative manner. At the beginning of the meeting, he had two individuals who were told to reach into a glass bowl that contained many folded pieces of paper. And on each piece, there was a positively charged word or phrase that had been written by him. After each one had read the words, the executive would state, "Those are the key words which will guide all of us in making this meeting not only productive, but also something that will guide us each day in becoming better managers."

This same executive was also great in using metaphors in meetings. Whenever conducting a staff meeting, your message will always get more attention and carry greater meaning when you verbally or visually illustrate it. We can take the old expression, "A picture is worth a thousand words," and extend it: "A metaphor is worth a thousand pictures." Also, remember that in order to effectively communicate a metaphor you need to use the proper cartoon, photo, illustration, or words.

## The Significance of Clarity

During one portion of our seminar, we asked the attendees what they disliked about staff meetings—what specific things irritated them. Their main complaint was in the "need-to-know" area. It was stated that at staff meetings, the senior managers who call the meetings often haphazardly communicate information. They too often monitor the information they disseminate in such a fashion that it is either partially confusing or totally misunderstood. And as a result of this, the staff members too often leave meetings confused on what specific actions to take or not take. It's somewhat like that joke about a boss who stated, "I know you think you know what I said; but it's not what I meant!" Unfortunately, that joke is real in some instances.

Besides communicating your message clearly, it is important to realize that in a staff meeting you're a "director" and not a "leader." The major difference between the two of them is that a leader often pulls, drags, or intimidates individuals to where the leader wants to go. She is like a person at the head of the line and everyone else is a duck in the row. A director points to which way she wants the group to go but is flexible enough to change the route if suggested by a follower. She is truly a team member who happens to be gifted at organizing the group.

## The Many Hats of the Manager

Lastly, we acknowledge that the manager's or executive's plate is full. She must wear many hats, and so we understand that adding "effective negotiator" to the list could be received with a little bit of dismay at first. But if we look more closely at several of those hats, it will become clear that negotiating has been part of the process all along. If you are in a managerial position, know that we're not adding another task to your agenda; we're saluting you for being willing to take on a role that inherently involves negotiating and we're helping you to see how much you do this every day! Moreover, our intention is to offer tips that will make your job easier, not more complicated. So let's look at a few aspects of being a manager, and note how central negotiating skills are to each role.

### The Arbitrator

One of the most important roles in management is when a manager must intervene in an argument, dispute, or any other situation that involves two or more individuals and is negatively affecting the business operation. A veteran and wise manager knows from experience when to listen to both sides of an argument and then make a decision or judgment that settles the issue, and when to listen and allow the individuals to settle it themselves after having received advice and counsel from the manager. Knowing the difference is very important and sometimes critical.

Whenever a manager settles the difference, one person is always dissatisfied. But when the matter is negotiated by the individuals themselves, there is a greater possibility of an "everybody wins" solution. Because the parties have settled their own differences without outside interference, they are likely to feel good about themselves and be more open to compromise and discussion in the future.

Unfortunately, we have known more than one executive who was blind to this method of negotiating conflict between employees. Such managers viewed their arbitrator roles like that of an official in professional athletics—as someone who calls balls and strikes or blows the whistle and ejects a player from the game because of poor conduct. However, there is a great difference between managing individuals in business and managing them at a sports event that is governed by strict rules.

We have all read about negotiations conducted between well-known athletes and the manager or owners of the teams they play for. It is not uncommon to hear that the parties in conflict reached a deadlock situation. In such negotiations, there is no referee or other official who steps in and settles the issue. The parties themselves, or their agents, have to do it. So we find ourselves pointing again to the fact that negotiating is not a game. It is a sophisticated human endeavor.

While it is not unusual in business for a manager to be put in the role of an arbitrator, the wise manager knows not to get stuck in a rut and try to resolve every situation in the same manner. A fundamental problem when negotiating in management is constantly playing the same role over and over again, instead of switching approaches based on the details of the situation. Managers sometimes do the same thing as actors and actresses—they typecast themselves, playing the same tactics time and time again.

## The Motivator

It is often very difficult to get someone to do something she doesn't want to do. It's even more difficult to change her mind about it. But those who are talented motivators can actually do just that. The great

Notre Dame University football coach Knute Rockne had the reputation of being a great motivator. It was rumored that he could motivate players to do incredible things. Once when asked by a reporter what type of football player he most preferred, he said, "If I tell a player to close a door in a room that has several open doors, I don't want him to ask me, 'Which door, Coach?' I want him to close all the doors and then ask, 'Any more doors, Coach?'"

One of the main jobs that a good manager/executive must fulfill is that of motivating the team. Incidentally, we believe that it is impossible to be an effective motivator without having excellent communication skills. The manager must clearly understand that communication is a dialogue, that it's not one-sided. Whether we like it or not, the message is in the receiver, not in the sender. Whatever a person hears is the real message, and not what you think you said.

If you want to be the best communicator and motivator that you can be—and thus the best negotiator that you can be—it is also essential to understand that communication involves more than that which is spoken. The reason for this is because every message is also affected by the context and the manner in which it is transmitted. Consequently, effective communication depends more on the attitude of the sender toward the receiver and the congruent nonverbal messages that accompany it.

For example, imagine that a manager attempts to communicate a message of praise and goodwill to someone who reports to her. However, as she delivers that message she has a scowl on her face and tightly crosses her arms on her chest. Let's face it—whatever she says will not come across as honest and sincere.

There are many motivational strategies that exist in management—bonus money, promotions, public recognition, company perks, even threats, just to name a few. And an experienced manager clearly recognizes that any one of them does not work for motivating everyone in the company. As the old expression states, "Different strokes for different folks!" What we do know is that the capitalistic system has learned that previous assumptions about employee motivation are no longer valid. At one time, the preservation of income was enough, motivating people to work harder simply to retain their jobs. But income has become solely an economic need, rather than a mixed economic/psychological factor. Once we understand the nature of what motivates individuals *today,* we can make some progress towards discovering new and perhaps better methods of motivating others.

In short, people are subject to a much more varied and much less stable set of influences than ever before. Local traditions and conventional wisdom are no longer the chief determinants of an individual's ideas and needs. Although human nature has not changed, the information available for shaping ideas and the world has had profound changes. And this trend will most likely accelerate. Therefore, in management it would be wise to forget the good-old-days. They are gone forever! Managers must become creative motivators, and that means making staff members feel that they are heard, cherished, and even mobile as far as company standing is concerned.

The fundamental factor in motivation is to realize that we are all basically self-centered to such a degree that we enjoy being praised, admired, respected, liked, loved, and accepted. And we also generally think of ourselves as having something to contribute to another person, family, friends, organizations, and mankind. As a manager, you must negotiate with the staff members so that the company wins access to their best skills and performances, and they win satisfying rewards for offering their best skills and performances.

## The Persuader

A manager also has to be persuasive. In order to motivate and direct others in accomplishing objectives, she must persuade them that whatever they have to do is necessary and important. And one of the greatest persuasion tools in the management kit is needs—just as they are at the negotiating table!

An excellent example of persuasive skills using needs to good advantage is found in how Michael Farraday acquired the necessary funds he needed from the British Government for his invention of the electric motor. He had made an appointment with Prime Minister William Gladstone and was allowed only a few minutes in which to obtain monetary approval for his project. He also clearly understood that intellect, logic, and statistical evidence do not persuade individuals—emotions and needs do! Shortly after they met and the necessary introductions were made, Farraday wisely awaited for the Prime Minister to speak first. Gladstone asked him in a very harsh, gruff voice, "What are the benefits of your invention, Mr. Farraday?" At this point, Farraday could have easily told Gladstone about all the great and wonderful things an electric motor would do for society. However, instead of describing what an electric motor would achieve, Farraday answered the question in an unexpected manner.

Farraday understood that, in many instances, people do things to satisfy their own needs, not necessarily someone else's. Therefore, Farraday responded in a loud and clear voice, "You'll be able to tax it!" He had put the government's need before his own and those of society. And since every government in the world is always looking for additional sources of revenue, the response from the Prime Minister was, "How much do you need?"

Whenever you're the persuader within your own company, business, or even family, it is very important to remember that another person does not buy your concept, idea, product, or opinion; they buy what it may or can do for them. Furthermore, in order for others to be persuaded, they must first be unhappy with their present situation and, second, pleased with what you have told and described to them. Persuasion always seems to work best when used on individuals who have reached a point in which change has to be made in their environment or life. And clearly, you can see how this is the very same set of conditions that are present at professional negotiations with other parties.

## The Terminator

The job of firing is often very difficult to negotiate. It is especially difficult when you must terminate individuals whom you have known for many years and with whom you have developed a close working relationship. By applying the same skills you would use at the negotiation table with an outside party, you can be quite effective. Just remember, you want to take the approach that no none walks away empty-handed.

Hank recalls an executive in the aerospace industry who was an outstanding negotiator at both hiring and firing. He especially remembers an occasion when the firm received a cancellation notice from the Department of Defense that necessitated a reduction in workforce. Hank's office was close to the executive's office and he was able to see individuals as they walked into the office to hear the bad news. He also saw them when they walked out, and many of them stopped by Hank's desk to say goodbye. Hank was amazed how many of them had smiles on their faces instead of appearing sad and unhappy.

A few days afterwards, while having lunch with his boss, Hank remarked, "You sure know how to practice the art of firing people!" The response was, "What the hell do you mean?" Hank then told the executive about the many individuals who stopped at his own office and talked. He mentioned that most of them were upbeat and didn't seem crushed by the news they had received. The executive then gave Hank some wonderful information on the art of firing people, especially under the circumstances in which he had to do it.

Whenever a termination is handled poorly, it can be devastating—not only to the individual, but to the entire department. It is very important to let people go with integrity and sensitivity because a poorly handled dismissal can cause greater amounts of hurt feelings and negative emotions that one realizes. As labor lawyers and business consultants often state, "A bad firing is bad business!" At worst, a bad firing can lead to lawsuits, sabotage, and even an occasional homicide. At best, a poorly negotiated dismissal can devastate department/section morale and the employees that remain.

So there are some fundamental principles to follow. If you are a manager or executive, you shouldn't delegate the responsibilities of hiring and firing to others. Do the job personally. The athletic director of a well-known university once fired the head football coach by leaving him a telephone message. And there have even been some managers who have terminated employees by e-mail. This benefits no one. We once read in the newspaper about a famous individual who invited one of his assistants out to lunch and gave him the termination notification after they had ordered dessert. The employee was so angry that he threw a piece of pie with ice cream at his former boss's face. And then the newly fired person revealed, "I've always wanted to do that; thanks for the opportunity."

In some instances, a dismissal is accompanied by a severance package and a notification that the firm's human resources department will stay in touch and assist in any new employment opportunities. This is very reassuring since the person still feels a certain connection when they depart. A manager, when negotiating the dismissal of an employee, must realize that the fired person is likely to undergo a certain amount of psychological shock. It is faintly similar to experiencing the death of a friend or the tragedy of divorce. Therefore, compassionate understanding will make the negotiating process much easier.

In summary, there are many roles a manager takes on during her business career, and they are roles that involve negotiating. Our primary reason for dwelling on the manager's or executive's role is to acknowledge that such an individual must pay equal attention to negotiating internally as she does externally. The manager *is* part of the team, not above the team or ahead of the team. Whenever there is a problem, dispute, issue, difference, or anything that needs to be discussed and resolved, the manager must take the lead in negotiating it in order to satisfy the needs of the individuals who are involved.

## NEGOTIATING AS A TEAM MEMBER

Now that we've examined the role of the manager, let's broaden the lens and include the whole team. A company's staff members must work well together in order for success to be achieved and morale to be high. *Teamwork* can be defined as the work accomplished by a group of associates or co-workers, each individual taking a part and working predominantly toward the established goals of the group rather than simply personal gain. Actually, teamwork is precisely how human beings, as a species, have accomplished so much. Henry Ford described teamwork in the following way: "Coming together is a beginning, staying together is a process, working together is success!"

Hank has often mentioned that when he first started conducting seminars on negotiating during the early 1960s, most of his family, friends, and business associates believed his work was primarily related to labor and management situations. He had to remind them that individuals constantly have to negotiate matters not only in business but also with family and friends. There are countless situations, professional and personal, in which there is conflict or differences that need to be resolved.

Whenever the word *teamwork* is used in a conversation, the speaker seldomly believes she needs to explain its meaning to another person. And yet like so many other words in the English language, many of us know so little about the substance of the word—the fundamental process, how it functions, and its importance in our lives. But if you are a member of a negotiating team, or even just a member of a company or business, you should definitely read this section on how to negotiate being the most effective part of that team that you can be.

Hank tells a funny story about what once happened at the end of a two-day seminar on negotiating. One of the attendees came up to him and said, "Thanks for a wonderful two days of explaining to me what I know, but didn't know I knew!" And that is precisely the purpose of this section on negotiating and teamwork. So let's tackle the four building blocks of teamwork when negotiating: leadership, communication, collaboration, and creativity.

## Leadership

Everyone would probably agree that in order to achieve effective teamwork, a leader or leaders must exist for purposes of keeping the team focused and avoiding losing sight of the goal(s). The methods a leader chooses to use may differ greatly from another leader's choices. For example, one might use a baseball bat, as Robert De Niro did in his role as Al Capone in *The Untouchables*. He lectured his gang members on the subject of teamwork as he led them by intimidation. Another leader may use compassion and lead by example, as Mother Theresa did for the members of her religious order. Although one used force and fear, and the other tenderness and love, they both achieved their objectives and were very successful leaders.

Indeed, the two styles mentioned above were efficient for their own purposes. But in today's world, there are so many other methods a leader may use. In fact, there are numerous books available on leadership. The one interesting aspect of all the books written is that a team leader's people skills—and, thus, negotiation skills—are often subordinated to those skills that bring profits to an organization. And as we have all seen, heard, and read, leaders who are not in touch with the consensus of the entire team set themselves and the organization on a course of failure.

In our individualistic society it can be extremely difficult to subordinate personal needs to the needs of the group or the whole. A principle reason for this is the strong survival drive that exists in each person—we are convinced that our needs are more important than the needs of others. It is not unusual for an individual to sometimes feel as though her needs may have been lost for the sake of achieving a team goal. A wise leader fully understands this and convinces the team that although the individual members may have lost something on an individual scale, each one has gained considerably more as the result of joining and becoming part of a greater effort.

An excellent example of this in history is how Roman leaders convinced defeated nations that losing in battle would become beneficial to them. After successful military conquests, Roman generals always made sure that a conquered nation clearly understood that although it may have lost a war, its people had become citizens of the Greater Roman Empire. And that, the Roman generals would argue, means protection, higher culture, and more.

If you are a leader, you probably don't necessarily want everyone within your authority to follow your instructions in a silent and dependent way. The majority of military historians seem to agree that during World War II, Adolf Hitler's campaign problems started when too many of his generals were team-players. As a result of this, there wasn't an honest or sincere assessment of their military plans during the invasion of Russia. As each battle was lost, there was no change in military strategy and tactics. Of course, the world is now grateful that those particular team members failed to be team leaders as well. But you can see what our point is.

As a leader of a negotiation team, there is absolutely nothing wrong with having the members of a negotiating team more often than not mutually agree on what course of action to take in a negotiation or what specific roles to play in it. If everyone follows a planned course of action like "trained ducks" and doesn't give honest and frank feedback to the chief negotiator, that team will have major problems.

Is it possible to share the weight of leadership? Yes, for whenever members of a negotiating team realize something is not working as planned, it's time to call for a break and talk things over. At such times it is very important for those who sense something is going wrong to convince the other members of that team that it is imperative to make changes and adjustments. That's teamwork. And all members of the team can be leaders in this way.

Unfortunately, there are times when chief negotiators have huge egos and are not in touch with the consensus of the entire team. Whenever this occurs, it usually sets the team up for ultimate failure in the negotiation. It is unfortunate that so many individuals around the world are unaware of how important teamwork is when negotiating. It brings individuals together and is the cement that bonds them in working for a common objective and outcome.

A very well-known individual who is C.E.O. of a major organization believes a team leader should select individuals for a team based on who will bring up opposing viewpoints and attitudes that force verification from the entire group. However, as he states, "Sometimes the outspoken 'devil's advocate' enjoys the role so much he refuses to give it up!" That's when a team leader must discreetly negotiate with the individual, either in front of the entire team or in a private meeting, to subordinate his feelings and beliefs in favor of the majority. Most team leaders are unaware they are "servomechanisms" and their major responsibility is keeping a team in line and on course, headed in the right direction.

Finally, one of the most difficult aspects of leadership concerns the loyalty of an individual. The loyalty an individual owes to the company and team is not inconsistent with the loyalty she owes to herself. A person needs to maintain and balance both in order to fulfill her personal ambitions while preserving her reputation as a good team-player. When both are in balance, a wonderful team negotiator exists. As a team leader, look for people who evidence such balance.

# Communication

Since passing notes between individuals during a negotiation is not recommended, we must speak in order to communicate what we're thinking. And when we do, three things can happen: (1) we say what we think we said; (2) what we say is not congruent with what we think; or (3) the message heard differs from what we really wanted to transmit to the others in the room.

Then, to add to whatever verbal communication may exist, there is nonverbal communication to consider. Sometimes it reinforces and compliments the verbal, and sometimes it contradicts it. Whenever the two are congruous, we tend to believe the message is genuine and sincere. And whenever they aren't, we tend to disbelieve what was stated. So be sure you are communicating to your team in an adequate manner—that you are not giving mixed signals, that you are expressing yourself clearly and genuinely, that you are aware of your body language as much as you are aware of your verbal language.

As a final thought on communication and the team, visualization is a key to opening up closed minds when communicating. Therefore, if you are capable of painting a clear "word picture" of your thoughts, those who hear them will also see a picture on the inner screen of their mind. So use descriptive language when possible. This will help you communicate well with your own team and with the other party in a negotiation.

# Collaboration

James Watson, who won a Nobel Prize with Francis Crick for the discovery of the double helix, stated, "Nothing new that is really interesting comes without collaboration!" Collaboration, much like a romance, is difficult to define. It may occur when a total stranger says something that triggers your thoughts and helps you instantly solve a perplexing problem. Or it may occur over a period of many years, in an ongoing relationship, such as in the situation of Rodgers and Hart who created wonderful musicals for their Broadway shows.

Collaboration is designed to produce results. Its principle purposes are to solve problems and to create or discover something new. In many team type negotiations, individuals have different specialized skills, expertise, or training. Each one is expected to contribute to the overall accomplishment of the team, like each player on a football team executes his skills, and as a result, the team scores a touchdown. The most interesting aspect of such contributions is that individuals don't necessarily have to like each other to succeed.

A classic example of this was the creative collaborative efforts of Gilbert and Sullivan, the famous composers and writers of comic operas in England. It was a well-known fact they both disliked each other, for they were very vocal in letting others know their respective feelings toward each other. However, they still managed to collaborate in creating great musicals that are still performed in England and the United States annually.

It is interesting that when individuals are assigned a task of working together towards a common goal, they seldom think about collaboration. We believe the reason is because most of us are cooperation-oriented and seldom think we are collaborating when interacting and contributing with others. Perhaps this is due to our early school training in which teachers emphasized cooperation or coordination with other classmates. It became normal and daily behavior for us.

In the numerous case-study negotiations we have recorded on videotape, we've discovered team collaboration blossoms in an unstructured and informal environment. That's a place where a person is comfortable enough to openly disagree, without fear of censure, and is also secure in voicing her opinion. What matters the most is that the individual has a feeling she is contributing something worthwhile and adding value to the negotiation.

## Creativity

Hank once asked a C.E.O. what his most important management function was, and the answer was very short and succinct: "My principle job in management is opening closed minds!" It is very natural for human beings to close their minds to anything they dislike, don't know, or don't have any interest in. Most of us enjoy surrounding ourselves with people and things that are familiar and comforting to us. And we often cast aside those things which are unknown, threatening, or frightening in any manner. But we believe the roots of creativity are revealed when, as Abraham Lincoln said, "we disengage ourselves from ingrained ways of thinking."

And that's when knowing about the N.I.H.-N.T.H. principle is important and necessary. There are few other things in life that block creativity and negotiations than this simple principle. The letters are verbal shorthand for "Not invented here. Not thought here!" In other words, since we didn't think about the concept, idea, method, etc., it must not be any good. This fundamental principle not only affects individuals, but also groups and organizations worldwide. And the effect on them is the same—it is a barrier to creativity.

We have conducted many seminars in Australia and New Zealand and once heard a classic example of creativity in how a power plant construction company received a contract. During their final round of negotiation with the customer, they were advised that if they could reduce the cost of housing construction workers at the building site, they would be awarded the contract. They spent several days carefully evaluating all the elements of cost, labor, material, transportation, supplies, equipment, and more in hopes of finding one or more areas where cost reduction might be possible. The one area they had not closely evaluated was the cost incurred in building a facility to house all the employees who would work and live at the project site.

And then someone, who was known as "Silent Sam" because he didn't talk a great deal, said in a quiet voice, "Let's buy a ship!" There was total silence in the room and he received a great number of stares from others who were probably thinking he was not playing with a full deck. After a few moments, the chief executive asked him, "What do you mean?" Sam quickly answered, "If we buy a ship and sail it to the site, we can live on it during construction. And afterwards, we can sell the ship, getting our costs for it back." How creative!

Due to the reduction of cost that the "ship plan" allowed, the company was awarded the construction contract. A ship was purchased as a capital investment, depreciated, and later sold when the construction project was completed. The team-player who thought of using a boat for housing truly practiced team spirit,

There are four steps to consider when developing an environment for team creativity before, during, and after negotiating. The first one is *problem definition*. It is amazing to us how many teams attempt to solve problems without first clearly defining them. For example, the sales manager of a major toothpaste company had called a meeting with her staff to discover why the previous month's sales had decreased. She was especially concerned because the sales of all their competitors had increased. There were eight regional managers attending, and each one had reasons for the decrease, ranging from the weather to the economy. At the conclusion of more than four hours, they finally properly defined their problem not as selling less than competitors but as needing to sell more toothpaste.

The second step is *incubation*. It is when the entire team is engaged in the process of coming up with ideas and suggestions. And in order for this phase to work well, we must remember the damaging N.I.H-N.T.H. principle covered earlier in this section. It is extremely important not to reject any idea regardless of how foolish it may seem. The period for eliminating ideas comes much later in the process. We should consider the second step as accumulating, not eliminating, creative ideas and concepts. Allow the ideas to flow and stop them only when you sense the well has gone dry.

The third step is *illumination*. That occurs when you, as a group, consider the best of the ideas and discuss them in more detail based on whatever production, sales and marketing, engineering, or other sources of information are available. It is also wise to discuss the validity, performance, and testing information of those sources and not overlook even what may be the most simple things, like a name or trademark.

General Motors learned this lesson the hard way many years ago, when it introduced the NOVA automobile. Their creative team-work yielded a group agreement that the name had a stellar ring to it and would be a surefire success. The one small detail they neglected was how the word would be accepted in other countries. In a few months they realized what a huge mistake they had made because the car was a complete bust in Mexico and in Central and South America. It was a complete surprise because the sales research conducted revealed the car would be a huge success in those areas. Further investigation for the failure disclosed that the word *nova* means "doesn't go" in Spanish. During the illumination phase, everything is important.

And the final step is *implementation*. It is the time for action, when a course must be laid out and planned. It is a time when we have to discuss who, what, where, when, and why—specific details. Such factors are critical for the implementation to work out well. Our recommendation for this phase is beware of taking shortcuts. Few things can cause a detour in your path to success as if you make something that is complex simple by merely rearranging matters.

This is also a good time to plan alternate methods, ways, and means of getting the job done. Remember the wisdom used when digging for well water: don't keep digging deeper in the same place. Instead, try another location.

We have worked through the elements of teamwork and highlighted the essentials for having an effective team. It is important to note that whether or not you are a manager/ executive, you can be a leader in your company. If you have mastered the art of negotiating internally, your daily work will show it—in the way you treat others, solve problems, come up with creative concepts, and speak up intelligently and respectfully. Others will notice that and follow your lead. You'll become the ultimate team player!

## CONCLUSION

After more than forty years of writing and lecturing on the subject of negotiating worldwide to thousands of managers and executives, as well as staff members, we have come to the realization that negotiation is one of the most important elements in teamwork. Negotiating brings individuals together and assists them in their efforts of working towards a common cause and objective. Confrontation alienates and separates them, often causing an "us" and "them" mentality among team members. So whether you are a team leader or not, a veteran or a new team player, an introvert or an extrovert, a presenter or a note-taker, take the information found in this chapter and apply it to your daily *internal* negotiations. Establishing excellent rapport and trust with your own team members will make it more likely that you'll establish excellent rapport and trust with the other party. And speaking of the other party, now let's turn to reading *those* individuals.

# 7

# How to Read Fellow Negotiators

## Nonverbal Clues and Gender Dynamics

*"What you are speaks so loudly,
I can't hear what you say!"*

—EMERSON

Finally, we'd like to share with you what we've learned about reading people and understanding people over the years. When people use the word *communication,* they usually assume that they're referencing spoken or written words. Similarly, when making decisions, discussing ideas, solving problems, and generally negotiating, we usually rely predominantly on words. We are primarily concerned with the verbal aspects of communication. However, in addition to that level of communication, there is a great amount of nonverbal information that is unconsciously transmitted between people.

As the above quotation by Emerson implies, the manner in which a person acts or behaves is often just as powerful as what he says. Furthermore, whenever there is contradiction between what someone states and his so-called body language, a person who is listening and looking will tend to believe that the true message is the nonverbal one, and so he tends to disregard the verbal message.

This chapter is concerned with how to read nonverbal communication. It is designed to make you a more observant negotiator. We'll start with facial expressions, which include everything from a flush to the blinking rate. The facial expressions a person makes can convey to an observant individual a great amount of information about what that first person is thinking and feeling—what is cooking in his "emotional pot." Then we'll study other nonverbal signals, such as sounds, silence, and gestures. But the scope of this part of the book is large; it is about reading people in numerous ways. So our final section will be on gender, for there are certain trends that exist in the way that men communicate and the way that women communicate. By the time you finish this chapter, you'll look at people in a whole new light! You'll rely on much more than what people say and you'll read them a lot more accurately.

## DECIPHERING NONVERBAL SIGNALS

In life and especially at every negotiation, nonverbal communication is not limited to obvious body language such as a roll of the eyes or a swing of the fist. There are subtle facial expressions, tell-tale sounds, loaded amounts of silence, and revealing gestures. For example, if someone said to you, "Believe me, I have an open mind regarding your proposal," yet said it while sitting in a chair with tensely raised shoulders and arms tightly crossed over the chest, you'd probably realize he is less than honest in the verbal remark he made. What you observed was that nonverbal communication often is more important than the words spoken.

The nonverbal cues are a great source for uncovering and understanding not only what the other party's true needs are but also, in some instances, what the other party is thinking. Developing these "reading skills" will make you a mental detective, a Sherlock Holmes of decoding other people. Nonverbal communication displays an individual's emotions and deep feelings. And since some of it is unconscious, the person is actually often unaware of what he is communicating nonverbally.

## Facial Expressions and Reactions

In his works of literature, the great Spanish writer Cervantes often referenced the power of messages conveyed in facial expressions.

One example is when the beloved character Don Quixote says to his friend Sancho Panza, "Note whether she changes color while you are giving her my message." Don Quixote is in love with a woman, Dulcinea, and he wants his friend to read her facial expressions, for that will reveal her true feelings.

The change in facial color that we know as "blushing" is caused by the arousal of the sympathetic nervous system, which dilates the small blood vessels of the face, ears, and neck, but not the rest of the body. It is a nonverbal clue that a person is feeling excited or agitated. So look for a flush in the faces of your fellow negotiators when you request information or disclose some of your own. If you notice blushing, you might want to consider that the reddening party is not being totally up-front or is burying an emotion that he doesn't think is appropriate at the time. Another possibility is that the tension is getting to him. Lastly but less common, the party could be very thrilled about what you just offered.

You might be questioning how valid face reading can be. Perhaps you are tempted to argue, "But great negotiators are great actors. They can cover their thoughts and feelings very well." True, some negotiators are great actors, but even they make slips that reveal their real feelings. Similarly, even great actors are not always in conscious control of what they are expressing. Let's look at an example.

In the acting profession there are times when an actor becomes so psychologically steeped in his character that he finds it difficult to turn the character off. The renowned actor Anthony Quinn experienced and described one such situation. He was traveling to Europe on a ship to perform the role of Quasimodo in the film *The Hunchback of Notre Dame*. The morning of the second day, he woke up, looked at himself in the mirror, and was shocked to see the entire side of his face distorted. It was as if he had suffered facial neuralgia overnight. Quinn quickly contacted the ship's doctor, who gave him some medication and told him not to worry. However, the next morning Quinn's face was still distorted. He saw the ship's doctor for a second time, and the doctor wisely came to the realization that something beyond his medical control was taking place. So he contacted a psychiatrist on board the ship for assistance.

Quinn then spent an hour with the psychiatrist, during which time he explained the purpose of his trip and how much time he had spent in attempting to get into the mindset of the character he would portray in the film. The psychiatrist smiled at him and said, "Tony, apparently you have done a great job of getting into your character because you are actually starting to look like him without the aid of any makeup. Now just relax and enjoy the rest of the voyage. Tomorrow morning, when you wake up and look at yourself in the mirror, everything will be all right."

The next morning Quinn found out the doctor was right; his face was no longer distorted. The moral of this story is that the face often reacts to emotional and psychological states without the person even realizing it. Mental energy can change a face significantly. As the great acting teacher Stanislavski often said, "If you can think about an emotion as hard as you can, the result will produce itself."

The only humans who are unable to read facial expressions are autistic children. Simon Baron-Cohen, who is an English expert on this disability, offers an interesting definition of the disorder: "It is the inability to put oneself in someone else's shoes and see the world from their perspective. Therefore, they are unable to interpret what a frown or raised eyebrow might mean."

Paul Eckman, who teaches at the University of San Francisco, is one of the foremost researchers in the study of facial expressions and has written several books on the subject. He believes facial expressions are a blend of several feelings and, because of this, are very difficult messages to understand clearly. This does not apply, however, to when a facial expression is used as a sign, like sticking out the tongue to signify playful distaste, or winking an eye as a sign of personal approval. Such gestures are intentional, clear messages that are culturally accepted ways to communicate a particular response.

Eckman believes an individual can became very adept at reading facial expressions with training. In fact, he has proven it with his Facial Affect Scoring Test (FAST). It is a system for measuring movements and expressions in several sections of the human face. The program has been designed for use by scientists and law-enforcement investigators. The training allows them to categorize facial behaviors based on the muscles that produce them and how muscular action is related to facial appearances. Eckman's FAST system has provided a standard measure of human facial gestures. It is the basis for most of the scientific discussion on what constitutes an expression, and what each expression might mean. We include this information to convince you that reading facial expressions is recognized as a valid way of assessing someone.

In addition to blushing, mentioned earlier, there are other facial expressions and reactions to look for. Some have to do with the eyes. It has been said that "the eyes are the mirrors of the soul." Then perhaps the eyes are important to observe. They can reveal a lot; that's the primary reason so many poker players wear dark glasses. Actually, they do so for three reasons: (1) to cover up their blink rate; (2) to hide the fact that, if they have light-colored eyes, their pupils will dilate when they peek at "two aces in the hole"; (3) to conceal when they glance at a player out of the side of the eyes.

What can you learn from eyeing someone's eyes? When a negotiation begins, your first observation should be in analyzing the normal blink rate of every individual, because later on it may prove to be very valuable information. At the start, people tend not to be nervous. Therefore, it is a wonderful period to determine what your fellow negotiators' normal blink rate is. Later on, when they are nervous, angry, lying, procrastinating, or the like, there will be a noticeable change in the blink rate. To a keen observer, it is as clear as a red light or green light when driving.

Whenever you enter the USA from a trip abroad, it is necessary to go through customs control. And the question every customs agent will always ask you is, "Do you have anything to declare?" When you undergo the process, notice how the agent always looks right into your eyes. The simple reason is to see how rapid your blink rate is. If your natural rate is above average, the agent will search every piece of luggage you have.

And custom inspectors are not the only ones in society who are concerned with blink rates for valuable information. Police inspectors, interrogators, psychologists, and psychiatrists also rely on them. They look for a change in the blink rate that might signify areas where a person is trying to cover something up or might be lying. Psychiatrists are especially aware of blink rates when they attempt to get personal information from a patient who is desperate to conceal it from them.

In addition to blushing and blinking, there are other facial expressions and reactions to consider. Facial tics can result from high tension, revealing that the person is uncomfortable with what's going on. So look for subtle tremors in the facial muscles. Moreover, the turning down of the corners of the mouth could signify displeasure or sadness. And the clenching of the teeth—or tightening of the jaw—tends to communicate frustration.

Believe it or not, there is no such thing as a "poker face," either in gambling or in negotiations. Every human unconsciously reveals his thoughts and feeling in some facial expression. The more you look for facial expressions and identify what they mean, the better you will be at getting the job of negotiator done.

## Sounds and Silence

Sounds may also nonverbally communicate how a person feels and thus reveal hidden emotions. The sounds we hear at negotiations fall into two categories: those that are made unconsciously, and those that are intentionally used to signal to fellow party members. Let's consider the intentional sounds first.

The island of Gomera is part of the Canary Island archipelago and has a population of 21,000 people. In addition to several spoken languages on the island, its inhabitants also use a nonverbal means of communication in which a series of whistles and chirps takes the place of sentences and entire paragraphs. The language is known as "Silbo," which comes from the Spanish word *silbar*, meaning "to whistle." It actually has four vowels and four consonants that can be strung together to form more than 4,000 words. Whenever two people communicate in Silbo, they sound like birds singing to each other. When negotiating, we can use the wisdom of Silbo to our advantage.

Both of us have been in negotiations in which the other side has contrived certain sounds to convey such messages as "Shut up," "Make it short," "Go in for the kill," and "It's your turn to talk." Although the sounds made are not whistles, they may be almost as loud—for example, the clearing of the throat or a specific pattern when tapping a pencil. So to be a very observant negotiator, you need to set your "nonverbal dials" to sound messages. And when you do, those codes that the other party has established will come through loudly and clearly.

Then there are the unintentional or uncontrollable sounds a nervous or uncomfortable person might make. Take, for example, a repetitive cough. Whenever a person has a genuine cough, due to a medical condition or allergies, you will hear it as soon as a negotiation begins. However, when it erupts well into the negotiation, a cough may signal a significant amount of nervousness, insecurity, or perhaps the state of being unsure. This type of cough usually is heard when the individual is speaking, and seldom when listening. It might be buying him time as he desperately attempts to come up with more to say, or it might be the result of dry throat from anxiety. Repetitive clearing of the throat functions in the same way.

There are many other unintentional sounds that you might pick up on now that you are tuned into such keen observance. A restless tapping of a pencil or foot communicates anxiety and frustration. Some people click or tap their nails in an attempt to appear more relaxed and confident than they actually are. Finally, you might know people who click their tongue against the roof of their mouth when they are deep in thought and trying hard to come up with a solution; it's an unconscious way to center their concentration.

It would be irresponsible for us not to mention silence in this section on sound and nonverbal communication. Silence, or the absence of sound, is just as much a language as words are! Of course, a respectful negotiator will be silent while another party is speaking; that's part of listening well. But when there are extended pauses or awkwardly long bouts of silence when a negotiator is supposed to be taking part in a give-and-take, clearly there is something awry. That tight-lipped person is struggling to make sense of what has just occurred and then to respond accordingly. There are two possibilities: (1) what you just argued was either convoluted or unexpected; (2) the silent party is losing ground and at a loss concerning how to handle it. You have to be the judge of which one more likely applies.

# Gestures

Another dimension of nonverbal communication involves gestures. Tell-tale gestures can occur while a person is speaking or while he is listening. Both areas are significant.

When a person is speaking, gestures that are congruent to the spoken words add additional emphasis to the point made; they embellish what is said. For example, a person might use a "karate chop"-type gesture or pound a fist on the palm of his other hand as if he were driving a nail with a hammer. These gestures are often used by someone who is very angry, emotional, and intent on driving home an important point.

There are very simple gestures that can communicate interest and respect. When a person's head is tilted while you are speaking, it means that he is eager to listen to your words. That's why we have the expression, "Lend an ear." And the gentle turning up and opening of the palms while speaking signifies that the person is open to the current conversation and willing to trade thoughts.

Incongruent gestures tip you off that there is some kind of dishonesty or cover-up occurring. Recall the example we previously used about a person who says, "Believe me, I have an open mind," and then tightly crosses his arms over his chest. Incongruent gestures and posture when a person is speaking require your attention and interest in order to determine which one of the contradictory messages is the true one—the verbal or the nonverbal.

Some people struggle with evaluating nonverbal messages because they are not allowing their intuitive instincts to influence them. The best definition we have ever heard to describe *intuition* is, "What you know for certain, but not for sure!" In our society, there is belief that women exercise their intuition much better than men do, and that they also observe small details much more. Whenever women are part of your negotiating team, make it a point to allow them to speak first when your team is discussing matters during a break. Allow them to express their perceptions made and how they view situations and individuals. Later on, you'll be thankful that you not only listened to what they said, but also that you followed their advice and guidance. There's a lot more on gender in the next section.

One caution: don't quickly leap to too many assumptions about the facial expressions, sounds, and gestures you witness. Use prudence before acting on something you think was just communicated through a facial tick, a code sound, or a hand movement, for example. Look for repetition and patterns before coming to a firm conclusion. The following story should alert you, in a humorous way, that one can make wrong assumptions.

Hank was on a business trip in Paris. The hotel he stayed in was very old and had paper-thin walls. He was awakened at 2:00 AM by the sound of two people who were expressing their love to each other in a physical manner. Since he was in Paris, he assumed it was a young, newly married couple and shortly went back to sleep. However, they woke him up again a couple of hours later with their love-making.

The next morning, after room service brought Hank coffee and sweet rolls, he walked out on the balcony and sat down to eat. Shortly, the French doors of the adjoining room opened and, to his surprise, out walked a man and a woman who were in their late 70s or early 80s. They bade him "bonjour" with great big smiles on their faces.

## STUDYING GENDER

The first corporate-sponsored seminar for managers and executives we conducted in which we used videotape recording equipment was in the 1960s, when Sony Corporation initially sold their portable video cameras. We used the equipment for purposes of recording case-study material, which the attendees negotiated during the two-day program. It was an excellent means of recording specific positive and negative behavior that was conducted in the negotiation. Moreover, it was a wonderful opportunity to document the specific differences between male and female negotiators.

During the first two years, most of the seminars were principally attended by male company employees, since female executives and managers were much fewer in number than they are today. However, as time went by, we noticed more and more females in management positions at the seminars. In fact, because of the increase in numbers, it was necessary to write new case studies that included women in negotiating roles. We used such studies whenever we had two or more females in attendance.

We should also add that we decided to do two important things. The first was to ask those attending our seminar what differences they might have seen, heard, or sensed between the sexes. Second, we asked them to add their observations and information to the list we had compiled. As you can probably imagine, after a few years, we discovered many things. The following is the result of our informational harvest on noticeable gender differences in the realm of negotiations. Some of our findings may surprise you and smash any assumptions you have made about gender and negotiating.

## On Being Comfortable

The very first observation regarding gender that we made was that, in general, men are more uncomfortable negotiating with women than women are with men. And the question of "why" is overwhelmingly answered in the same way: because women have been negotiating with men in order to have their needs met since time immemorial—in castles, manors, households, and caves, for thousands and thousands of years. They have traditionally not been the physically bigger or stronger party, so they had to learn methods of expressing their needs and wants that went beyond simple intimidation. Perhaps this also explains why women are not drawn to domineering men, contrary to what many men seem to think.

Both sexes agreed that women seem to have a talent for instinctively knowing how to control men in ways other than direct verbal skills. The one most mentioned at our seminars is "reading men like a book." It appears that women seem to know exactly what some men are thinking by their body language. Generally, women are more aware of men's gestures, postures, facial expressions, and sounds. And that's a winning trait. During a negotiation, if one is capable of reading the other person's fundamental feelings, that reader has a huge advantage, for she can better anticipate what the other person is going to say or do.

# On Showing Aggression

We also discovered differences in the amount of hostile behavior displayed during negotiations. Men are clearly more openly hostile towards others and show it not only by raising their voices but also in other ways. We recorded instances in which they pounded the tabletop, broke objects like pencils, and generally behaved in a manner most women would not. Furthermore, in some cases such physical show was a clear expression of their frustration in trying to achieve the upper hand in the negotiation. At other times, it was a planned tactic to win through intimidation—an approach some negotiators have found difficult to abandon and are still using even though it seldom works as planned.

When a negotiation consists of both men and women, it is generally the males who tend to be more aggressive and want to control the negotiation and its direction. Overall, they tend to make most of the strong statements and also ask the majority of questions. In our seminars, we have advised women to take a more aggressive attitude when negotiating. We also mention that some male negotiators are impressed by females who "act like a man" and refuse to take subordinate roles. So we suggest that women not feel they will offend fellow negotiators by being more demonstrative.

There is an important point to make about being more verbal, however. There were times during our in-house seminars when negotiating teams recessed and we eavesdropped on their conversations for purposes of discovering what they discussed. It was very interesting to find that women who had had very little to say during the negotiation had a great deal to say during the recess. And also, the men in the groups listened very closely to what the women expressed. So women are certainly cherished team members, and they also like to converse in relaxed environments.

# On Emotions and Responses

What truly surprised us is that men tend to display more emotions than women do. Most men grow up thinking that women display their emotions more readily. And perhaps at certain times, such as at weddings and funerals, they may. But this does not hold true at negotiations.

Yet while men might be more emotionally expressive, women have "thin-skin" and are more sensitive than men when it comes to negative, critical, and intimidating remarks—especially when the comments are made by other women. Females tend not to handle such criticism as well as men do. We also noted something else very interesting. Whenever someone became very emotional and lost control, if there were women in the negotiation they were usually the ones who made an effort to calm or comfort the individual. However, when the group was completely male, very seldom did anyone make such an effort.

Hank comes from a family of nine—six men and three women—and has often remarked that it was his sisters who assisted in negotiating peace in the family, especially in a conflict between brothers. This has historical roots. For generations, women have played the role of peacemakers in society. Perhaps we might have had fewer large-scale wars if women had been in positions of power. The "gentler sex" has displayed a greater willingness in reaching agreements and settlements, and thus overcoming conflict, than men have. We are not relying on cultural judgments here; we have observed these tendencies in the hundreds of videotaped negotiations we have recorded over the years.

## On Humor

Male negotiators who are gifted with a great sense of humor are accustomed to using humor to handle harsh comments. And men, in general, seem to use humor more often. Indeed, as a general rule of conduct, women are much more serious when negotiating than men are, and they tend to tell far less jokes or introduce humor into the process.

Men find it easy during the entire process to interject humor or laugh at their situation, especially when in "muddy waters" and going nowhere fast. They are also more likely to be storytellers, using simple homilies that illustrate the direction the negotiation is taking. This occurs most frequently when everyone at the table feels the same way.

## On Compromise and Changing One's Mind

Women tend not to view making compromises as a weakness, but so many of the men with whom we have talked *do* see compromise as some form of weakness. Females appear to be more tuned in to the process of giving and getting. Furthermore, even when not receiving something in return, they largely view the compromise as "planting seeds" for use later and therefore ultimately getting something in return. While women seem to compromise more readily, men tend to debate issues more than women.

One finding that caused us no surprise whatsoever was that women are usually much more receptive and willing to change their minds on a position, issue, or other matters being discussed in a negotiation. We have all heard the expression, "It's a woman's privilege to change her mind!" So what we additionally learned was that they also know how to do it well! But we offer a strong warning: there are few tougher negotiators you will ever encounter than women who have reached a point at which they believe they have made sufficient compromises and are not receiving anything in return.

An experienced colleague of ours who has negotiated a variety of situations over many years has often stated, "It's okay to take positions, but never dig a hole so deep that you're unable to get out." Men seem to dig "beach-heads" for defensive purposes early during a negotiation and later find it very difficult to fill in the holes dug and change gears. Flexibility is important for successful negotiating.

## On Listening and Questioning

We observed that women are much better listeners than men. And as a result, they tend to interrupt the speaker less. Because they are much better listeners, they are capable of finding weaknesses in another person's argument or proposal. A negotiating team benefits greatly by including women because of this.

Women are also much better at reading nonverbal messages (body language) when negotiating—a different type of listening. They often see things that men sometimes have completely overlooked. Because of this innate ability, we believe that women have the ability of becoming expert poker players. And in viewing poker tournaments on television, we have noticed there are more women participating in them than there were a few years ago.

The same goes for questioning. Hank once conducted a seminar for police officers and one of them stated; "Women officers are better interrogators than men. It's a pity we don't use them more often when interrogating suspects." Their questions tend to be more productive in subtle ways. Also, women have learned a very valuable lesson: men, in general, are often impatient when they have to negotiate with women. This awareness has been a negotiating strength for women, for they have taken advantage of it by getting what they want by simply carrying matters to a point at which many males will give in to them.

## On Memory for Details

In general, women tend to spend more time discussing the background or history of a negotiating situation as they seek ways and means of resolving differences. And in the process, they seem to display an uncanny memory system through which they are capable of relating specific details, facts, and information. It is a capability that many men cannot seem to duplicate.

As an example of this, just ask any woman to recall the lyrics of a song she leaned to sing when she was very young. And then do the same to a man. Men usually remember the tune and may even be able to hum it, but they are usually very foggy when it comes to recalling the words. Women are not.

## On the Use of Data

There is, however, a difference favoring males when it comes to "crunching the numbers" and analyzing data. We found men better able to respond in situations requiring statistics, monetary projections, and other such matters. However, women seem capable of balancing the scales because they respond more favorably when it comes to alternatives, options, or other means of resolving differences or something that is being disputed. Males often quickly negate alternatives that may clash with what they offered or want instead of investigating them further. Women are experts when it comes to seeing some value in the merest of options; often picking them like they would the bones of a Thanksgiving turkey for later use in a soup.

The comparisons we have made are by no means intended to promote bias or make sweeping generalizations that confirm stereotypes. We are very careful to report only what we have found evidenced time and time again at our workshops. And we provide this information so that you can read others more accurately during negotiations, and treat them more appropriately. We also believe that this information will help you appreciate your own team members for their strengths and tendencies.

## CONCLUSION

Do you feel that you are now more prepared to read the behaviors of those across the negotiating table? Are you a little more confident with the gender dynamics in the room? We hope so. By becoming more aware of the subtle ways that humans communicate, we can all become better negotiators—at the office, at the conference center, at home. So when you are listening to what the other party has to say, or even working within your own party, check whether or not the nonverbal communication—in all its forms—is congruent with the verbal messages. Do the silent messages verify the spoken ones? And be sure to be respectful of gender differences and strengths. Remember, respectfulness is part of the successful negotiator's profile.

# 8

# Additional Considerations
## Misconceptions
## and Self-Assessments

*"Information is a negotiator's greatest weapon."*

—VICTOR KIAM

ook back at the task that was before you at the beginning of this book, and then pat yourself on the back for achieving such a comprehensive and productive study of the art of negotiation. You started with general fundamentals and basic human behavior, moved through information on how to be a successful negotiator and how to prepare for a successful negotiation, and finally considered more specific details on the people involved, from understanding your own role to reading the other people in the room. Is there anything left to consider?

It's true, we have almost completed our study of the art of negotiating, but we have two more areas to tackle before you tackle your next negotiation. As you ready yourself to embark on a new deal, we ask you to do two things. First, check that you are not falling prey to any of the common destructive myths about negotiating that we will review in this chapter. And second, set aside in a safe place this chapter's advice on how to assess yourself in a constructive manner that will wield an honest appraisal. That way, when you finish your negotiation, you will have at your fingertips reasonable tools by which to judge your work.

## CLARIFYING COMMON MISCONCEPTIONS

As you worked through the chapters of this book, you certainly put in the time and energy to develop a healthy attitude toward negotiating. But there are a lot of common myths or misconceptions out there that can charm you if you are not forewarned of their errors. So read through the following erroneous assumptions about negotiating and what makes the best negotiators. We not only point out four misconceptions but also discuss the specific reasons why each is not valid.

# Misconception #1

The first myth is that a strong negotiator is hard-nosed and uncompromising in pursuit of her goals and objectives. It is a great fallacy because, in most instances, those who take this approach and attitude are working against their own needs, hindering instead of helping their chances of success. They tend to be rigid and inflexible in their ability to explore alternatives that require any concessions or compromises. Such behavior increases the likelihood of an impasse. Moreover, that type of behavior creates major difficulties in overcoming an impasse because most of the attention is focused on winning only one party's objectives. Such lack of awareness of the other person's needs sorely affects persuasive abilities.

The negotiator who truly knows her strengths is rarely inflexible or uncompromising. In society, there is a misrepresentation of successful individuals—they are seen necessarily bull-headed. That's a distortion and exaggeration of a more tempered trait—persistence. A persistent person doesn't lose sight of her goals and objectives, but that does not mean she is stubbornly resistant to change or unyielding when it comes to making compromises or concessions.

# Misconception #2

The second misconception is that the strong negotiator is very secretive and divulges an absolute minimum amount of information to the other side during a negotiation. During our seminars in which we videotaped case-study negotiations, we discovered a very interesting dichotomy on this subject. When the attendees were questioned at the beginning of our two-day program, the majority stated they didn't believe disclosure was a weakness, or that secretiveness was necessarily a positive factor. However, when we played back the videotaped negotiations during which attendees were given confidential information to either share or withhold, we found there was a significant amount of important information that was not disclosed to the other party.

In discussions, we have heard many remarks by seminar attendees stating how they wished they had disclosed certain information because not having done so worked against their needs. Many negotiators simply have a tendency to hold onto exclusively known information because it makes them feel that they have some sort of power position as keepers of that information. The truth of the matter is that managing information effectively is where the real strength lies. And it begins in the preparation phase during which decisions are made relative to what will or will not be disclosed, and who will do the disclosing. We have acquired a file of analogies from the wisdom of seminar attendees. One effective analogy likens withholding information to being stingy: "Hoarding information is like hoarding money. It contributes little to a person's ultimate welfare!"

Negotiators who manage information best generally are experts at using incremental disclosure to their advantage. They recognize the value of information as a medium of exchange, and they wisely trade off pieces of it for information or concessions that have value to them. Of course, they also practice a policy of a certain amount of secretiveness because they realize that information is negotiable a single time only.

## Misconception #3

Another misconception in the field of negotiations is the belief that the individual who is talking is the one who is in control of the process. Actually, most of the time, the individual who is most talkative is actually the one who feels the need to desperately defend her needs, position, and issues. She is in over-compensation mode.

We spent a year reviewing the hundreds of case-study negotiations we videotaped for purposes of finding how evenly divided talking was in an average negotiation. And we discovered three very interesting things: (1) talking was evenly divided between the two sides, more or less nearly 50 percent each; (2) approximately 80 percent of the time, the speaking individual was explaining, demanding, or persuading; (3) the balance of time was spent asking and answering questions, disclosing information, getting agreements, making compromises, and settling.

In many negotiations, a person speaks because she is in the process of explaining something to the other party. The explanation grows out of a question that's been asked, or it may be an attempt to clarify a position taken on a particular issue. However, often the explanation is defensive in nature and hostile words are used that don't contribute anything towards developing a cooperative spirit between the two sides.

And then there are times when a person talks to persuade or sell the other side. But if there is one thing we have learned after many years of negotiating and conducting seminars on the subject, it is that negotiators are not great at selling to others. And the principle reason is that most are very poor listeners and have a tendency toward overkill. They fail at being "good closers," which is the major strength required of a person who sells. Those who oversell continue talking instead of asking for a signature. They have a tendency to rant on and on while the potential buyer begins to suspect that all the emphasis on positives is intended merely to cover up a negative.

There is also something else that experts at selling would not do, and that many negotiators constantly do. It is being "counter-oriented." By this we mean that many negotiators prepare themselves psychologically for encountering objections to what they say or ask for. As a result of this, they stop listening for responses that may indicate an opening presented for a possible compromise or concession. In other words, negotiators prepare themselves to have doors shut on them, whereas great salespeople expect closed doors and wait for a slight opening so that they can stick their foot in the door.

A major part of negotiating requires a person to take a defensive position on needs, issues, information, past performances, and more.

However, there is a huge difference between defending your position and making yourself look foolish or paranoid. And nothing can do so more quickly than talking too much while explaining something in a negotiation. Talkative individuals become less convincing the more they speak, and they are experts at "snatching defeat from the jaws of victory." The successful negotiator provides the most direct and succinct responses to any challenge posed by the other person. There's no compulsion to overwhelm the opposition with a flood of verbal "gobbledy-gook."

Harsh critics also tend to speak too much, and they often accomplish nothing more than irritating the other side. They undermine themselves by evoking resentment and resistance, which seldom motivates anyone into cooperating or making concessions. If we have learned anything about negotiating, it is "the tougher the tactics, the tougher the resistance."

## Misconception #4

And the final misconception is that when a proposal made is followed by a period of silence, the person who breaks the silence loses. In reality, the person who knows how to break a silence first is the one able to hold the initiative. Hank discovered this skillful maneuver years ago during a prolonged silent period in a negotiation. The other person looked at him and, with a slight smile on his face, stated, "I take your silence to mean you've just agreed with everything I've said!" That man had taken silence as a nonverbal message of acquiescence and agreement, and he showed no fear whatsoever that breaking the silence was a sign of weakness.

Hank has used that same expression in other negotiations and reports it works well. There are times when the other person will affirm the remark, and times when she will state, "Like hell it is!" In either case, breaking the silence in such a way doesn't reveal weakness, so don't be afraid of doing so.

Did any of these misconceptions sound reasonable at first? Were you susceptible to one or two of them when you first read them? If so, don't feel disappointed in or frustrated with yourself. Even veteran negotiators can fall for these myths because they are misconceptions that have been purported for many years. But now you know the truth, and now you have an excellent understanding of the truth and the lies behind what makes a great negotiator. All that's left to do is to sharpen your self-assessment skills.

## THE SUMMARIZATION PROCESS

The outcome of every negotiation you have ever conducted and every negotiation that you will ever conduct falls into one of three possible conclusions. The first possibility is that you are highly satisfied with what you accomplished—the goals and objectives achieved. Next, you could be totally dissatisfied with the outcome and feel as though you failed in achieving the goals and objectives you sought. Lastly, you might experience emotional feelings that fall in-between the two situations just mentioned. Whichever category you find yourself in, you should conduct an assessment to see what went right and what could be improved.

In our negotiating seminars we have asked attendees a few questions relative to their thoughts and feelings concerning the conclusion of a negotiation. The overwhelming number of respondents has stated that if they achieved most or all of their goals and objectives, they went on and celebrated, sometimes getting drunk with joy. And when they didn't meet their expectations, some got drunk on something other than joy! What is absolutely amazing is that, for the most part, people have admitted they don't really learn from the mistakes they make.

Both of us find a great value in conducting thorough and honest assessments of our work and then making well-planned changes as a result. Many years ago, when we started conducting seminars, we reviewed not only the comments attendees gave us regarding the value of our program, but we also mutually discussed what seemed to go over well and what didn't. As a result of this, we improved the course content and added or eliminated certain jokes and stories.

We truly believe that, after its conclusion, every negotiation session should be analyzed. Note, we say after every *session*, not just at the end of the negotiation. This allows the negotiators to tweak their skills and expand their repertoires. The best way to self-assess is to discuss the day's work with fellow negotiators from your party. Instead of heading for the nearest bar for a drink, head for the nearest office or conference room and talk about what has occurred. Cover as many of the following points as necessary.

- What was the day's outcome? Did anyone summarize it so that both sides left the negotiation with the same views?

- Are you pleased with the day's effort? If not, where could you have done better?

- Are there any areas in which you need additional information or clarification? If so, make sure to get such information at the beginning of your next meeting with the other party.

- If you didn't get any firm agreements or settlements, did you get any agreements-in-principle? If you did, what were they? Did you recap them so the other side understood them well?

- Looking back on the negotiation, can you recall a specific positive or negative point that greatly influenced whatever agreements were mutually reached?

- If the time allotted for the negation had been extended, do you believe you might have reached a settlement or better agreement? If so, how much more time do you believe was necessary?

- If you had the entire day to do all over again, would you change anything you did or said?

- Were there any unexpected surprises in what individuals said or did? If so, what were they?

- Were there any concessions made? Who made the first one? Did you write it down or repeat it verbally? What was the initial response to concessions made? Did the reactions surprise you?

- During your preparation, did you discuss what the initial concession would be and who would make it?

- Did either side disclose any important information? What was it, and what was the effect when it was disclosed?

- Did the other side seem to believe your disclosure, or did they show doubt?

- Did either side have a disruptive person whose behavior negatively influenced the negotiation? Did anyone make an attempt to curb that person's comments and behavior?

- How many questions do you recall asking and answering? Which ones were expected? Which ones were not?

- Where there any breaks or recesses called, and if so, who requested them? Were there any offers, counters, disclosures, or other information revealed afterwards?

- Were there any threats or implied threats made by either side? If so, what were they and who made them?

- Did you fundamentally follow the preparations made? If not, what changes did you make, and what were the results?

- Were there any concessions you planned to make but didn't? If so, what were they and do you still plan on making them?

- Would you like to negotiate with the person/s again? If not, why?

After going through this list of questions, have each person who was engaged in the negotiation describe it in her own words—what she learned, what she would do differently, and what needs to be changed before the next meeting with the other party under discussion or before the next negotiation in general.

If you were the sole negotiator and do not have co-workers who would be interested in or invested in listening to you assess the job, go through this list yourself. Take notes on your own performance, what worked and what didn't. Perhaps you could even ask a friend—one whose intellect and opinions are respectable and reliable—to hear you out and give you some honest feedback. The important part is that you are reviewing your work with an open mind and a constructive attitude.

# CONCLUSION

Congratulations! You have finished you own brief course on *the art of negotiation*. We hope you have enjoyed the discussions on everything from the big gestures to the subtle nuances. Always remember to enter into a negotiation relationship with a cooperative spirit. Don't underestimate the importance of good preparation. And always keenly observe others. Most of all, enjoy your work as a negotiator, for there's no better service than to actively lay the foundation so that two parties can build a mutual trust and fulfill their individual needs.

# Conclusion

*"Art does not solve problems but makes us aware
of their existence. It opens our eyes to see
and our brain to imagine."*

—Magdalena Abakanowicz

We hope that, as you read through the chapters of this book, you found yourself revisiting old issues, creating new strategies, and most important, looking forward to your next negotiation. After all, to be a truly successful negotiator, you have to like what you do. When you find your daily tasks stimulating and productive, it shows on your face, through your gestures, and in your work.

The fact that you dedicated the time to read this book is a testament to your commitment to *the art of negotiating.* And it certainly was not wasted time. You have gained quite a collection of information on the principles, the processes, and the personalities of negotiations. In fact, there were too many valid points to summarize all of them here. In the pages of this book, we have touted the cooperative approach to negotiating and urged you personally to try new tactics. We have challenged you to self-analyze and encouraged you to read others more closely. We have structured a preparation plan and torn down lingering myths about negotiating. Certainly, you are ready to tackle your next negotiation with confidence.

When they hear the word *negotiation,* a great number of people think of pressure-laden court situations or dry, obligatory business meetings. We have tried to erase that stereotype and put a positive, exciting attitude back into the term. And we have also kept the word *art* in prominent view because we firmly believe that skillful negotiating is a creative endeavor. So our parting suggestions to you are ones that could just as easily be offered in a sculpture or painting workshop, at a piano recital, or backstage before belting an aria:

Let your character, creativity, and passion shine. Engage others with your work. You never know how many people you will change through your efforts. And remember, while you can't control how everyone responds to your work, you *can* have peace of mind that you gave it your all.

# About the Authors

**Gerard I. Nierenberg,** a successful lawyer, was one of the first people to realize the role negotiation plays in resolving disputes—both personal and business-related. He pioneered the idea of the "everybody wins" philosophy—now usually referred to as "win-win"—which insures that all parties benefit from the negotiation, as opposed to the "winner takes all" approach. In 1966, he founded the Negotiation Institute, a not-for-profit organization that offers state-of-the-art training to business and professional organizations, governments, and executives around the world. Dubbed "The Father of Negotiation Training" by *Forbes* and one of the "Eight Wise Men" by *The Wall Street Journal*, Nierenberg has written over twenty best-selling books on negotiation and related subjects, including *Earn From Your Mistakes, The Complete Negotiator,* and *Fundamentals of Negotiating.* His books have been translated into over thirty languages. He and his wife currently reside in New York City.

**Henry H. Calero** has been writing about communication and negotiation for over thirty years. He is the former president of C-M Associates, a management consulting firm that specializes in conducting seminars on negotiation, interpersonal relations, and communication. A consultant and writer for professional, academic, and technical publications, he is also the co-author of *How to Read a Person Like a Book* and *MetaTalk* with Nierenberg. Some of his books include *Winning the Negotiation, Negotiate the Deal You Want,* and *The Human Side of Negotiating.* He currently resides in California, in the greater San Francisco area.

# Index

Adler, Alfred, writings on power structure by, 100

Advantage, gaining of, as way of clarifying preconditions, 83. *See also* Preconditions, clarification of, when preparing for negotiation.

Agent of limited authority, as negotiating technique, 113–114. *See also* Negotiating, techniques for.

Agreements-in-principle
attempt to secure, as way of overcoming an impasse, 117
consideration of, in preparation for negotiation, 95–96
*See also* Impasse, ways to overcome; Writers' strike (2007–2008).

American Labor Party (ALP), use of reversal technique by, 107

Apparent withdrawal as negotiating technique, 105–106. *See also* Negotiating, techniques for.

Assistance, needing of, to solve problem, as way of clarifying preconditions, 82. *See also* Preconditions, clarification of, when preparing for negotiation.

Association as negotiating technique, 109–110. *See also* Negotiating, techniques for.

Assumptions
as example of what not to do, 126–131
favorable, 131–132

Bacon, Francis, "Of Negotiating," essay by, 81

Barnett, Lincoln, thoughts of, on knowing thyself, 77

Baron-Cohen, Simon, studies on autism and facial expressions by, 160

Baruch, Bernard, example of reversal negotiating technique by, 106–107

Behavior
predicting, 22–25

Determination of what will be lost as way of overcoming impasse, 115–116. *See also* Impasse, ways to overcome.

Diagram of differences as way of overcoming impasse, 120–121. *See also* Impasse, ways to overcome.

Disclosure, making a, as way of overcoming impasse, 118–119. *See also* Impasse, ways to overcome.

Displacement as standard type of behavior, 33. *See also* Behavior, standard types of.

Disraeli, Benjamin, 104

Disassociation as negotiating technique, 110. *See also* Negotiating, techniques for.

Discussion

of good association as way of overcoming impasse, 122

of remaining alternatives as way of overcoming impasse, 118

*See also* Impasse, ways to overcome.

Donne, John, 27

Eckman, Paul

Facial Affect Scoring Test (FAST), 160–161

research on facial expressions, 160–161

Ego, effects of, on negotiating, 136

Emotions, role of, in motivation, 40–42

Empathy, asking for or offering, as way of overcoming impasse, 119–120. *See also* Impasse, ways to overcome.

Environment, importance of relaxed, 138

Expression of feelings as way of overcoming impasse, 116. *See also* Impasse, ways to overcome.

Facial Affect Scoring Test (FAST). *See* Eckman, Paul, Facial Affect Scoring Test (FAST).

Fait Accompli as negotiating technique, 104–105. *See also* Negotiating, techniques for.

Farraday, Michael, use of persuasion by, 144–145

Favor, looking for, as way of clarifying preconditions, 83. *See also* Preconditions, clarification of, when preparing for negotiation.

Feinting as negotiating technique, 109. *See also* Negotiating, techniques for.

Forbearance as negotiating technique, 102–103. *See also* Negotiating, techniques for; Quakers, the, use of forbearance by; Roosevelt, Franklin D.

Forbes, Malcom, expression of power by, 43

Ford, Henry, description of teamwork by, 147

Freud, Sigmund

as father of psychoanalysis, 93–94

reputation as a great motivator,
142–143
Rodgers and Hart, as example of
collaboration, 151
Rogers, Carl, 55
Role playing as standard type of
behavior, 34–36. *See also*
Behavior, standard types of.
Roman Catholic Church. *See*
Psychodrama, Roman
Catholic Church's use of.
Roosevelt, Franklin D., 10
story about forbearance, 103

St. Peter's Church. *See* Citicorp,
negotiation with St. Peter's
Church.
Salami as negotiating technique,
112. *See also* Negotiating,
techniques for.
Saxe, John Godfrey, "The Blind
Men and the Elephant," story
by, 58–59
Self-assessment. *See* Negotiator,
self-assessment of.
Setting limits as negotiating
technique, 108–109. *See also*
Negotiating, techniques for.
Shaw, Bernard, 33
Silbo. *See* Nonverbal signals,
sounds and silence.
Silence as negotiating technique,
103–104. *See also* Negotiating,
techniques for; Nonverbal
signals, sounds and silence.

Sounds
intentional, 162–163
unintentional, 163
*See also* Nonverbal signals,
sounds and silence.
Stanislavski, thoughts of, on
facial expressions, 160
Subject, changing of, as way of
overcoming impasse, 116–117.
*See also* Impasse, ways to
overcome.
Surprise as negotiating technique,
104. *See also* Negotiating,
techniques for.

Threat, managing of, as way of
clarifying preconditions, 83.
*See also* Preconditions,
clarification of, when
preparing for negotiation.

*Understanding Human Nature*
(Adler), 127
*Untouchables, The*, as an example
of leadership, 148
U.S. Customs Authority, as
example of good use of
assumptions, 131–132

Watson, James, thoughts of, on
collaboration, 151
Writers' strike (2007–2008), as
example of agreement-in-
principle, 95–96, 133

# ABOUT
# THE NEGOTIATION INSTITUTE

The Negotiation Institute, formed in 1966 by Gerard I. Nierenberg, is the pioneer organization devoted to the study of negotiation and related fields. The Institute offers state-of-the-art training to governments, executives, businesses, and educational organizations around the world. To date, over 1 million people have attended the sessions.

Since its origination, the Negotiation Institute has provided the world's most well-known and respected negotiation training seminars. Its clients include some of the largest national and international businesses and industries, local and regional governments, universities, colleges, and other educational institutions, as well as dozens of associations. Some of the Institute's more well-known clients include: Sony, Ford Motors Company, Burger King, Nabisco, Inc., IBM, Inc., Citigroup, Sears, Pfizer, the Food and Drug Administration (FDA), the Federal Aviation Administration (FAA), and the American Medical Association (AMA) banks.

The Institute conducts its programs internationally. It is also a Non-Governmental Organization member of the United Nations. In the past, when the Institute was a law firm, it represented such countries as Bangladesh, Cameroon, and Kenya. The Declaration of Independence for Bangladesh was signed at the Negotiation Institute's office. The Institute specializes in on-site seminars for five or more people. Each seminar is created specifically for the needs of the specific organization. Seminar lengths range from short keynote speeches to five-day intensive training programs.

Seminars can work wonders on both the individuals who attend and the organization as a whole. Individually, attendees will learn to make better deals, both in a business environment and in their personal lives. Businesses as a whole will benefit from a smoothly functional organization whose departments cooperate with each other to gain maximum beneficial results for the company. Everybody Wins® is both the aim and the result of attending the Art of Negotiating® seminar.

For more information, visit the Institute's website:

## www.negotiation.com

Or call the Institute: (212) 888-0053

# HOW TO READ A PERSON LIKE A BOOK

Using Body Language to Know
What People Are Thinking

Gerard I. Nierenberg, Henry H. Calero, and Gabriel Grayson

Imagine meeting someone for the first time, and within minutes—without a word being said—having the ability to accurately know what that person is thinking. Magic? Not quite. Whether we are aware of it or not, our body movements clearly express our feelings, attitudes, and motives. The simple gestures that we normally pay so little attention to can communicate key information—information that can be useful in so many situations. *How to Read a Person Like a Book* is designed to teach you how to read and reply to the nonverbal signals from business associates, friends, loved ones, and even strangers. Best-selling authors and expert negotiators Nierenberg, Calero, and Grayson have collaborated to put their working knowledge of body language into this practical guide to recognizing and understanding body movements.

*$15.95 • 224 pages • 6 x 9-inch quality paperback • ISBN 978-0-7570-0134-1*

# INVESTIGATIVE SELLING

How to Master the Art, Science & Skills of Professional Selling

Omar Periu

Within each super salesperson is an expert detective, as skilled as Sherlock Holmes. For a lucky few, these sleuthing talents come naturally, but for most, these skills must be learned—and it is these skills that turn the average salesperson into the master seller. Now, Omar Periu, nationally renowned "high energy" sales trainer, provides readers with the secrets of becoming a top sales professional in *Investigative Selling*.

Like any good investigation, selling begins with observation, questioning, and listening. *Investigative Selling* not only details these skills, but also explains the most effective way to use the information you gather. And it applies investigative selling techniques to a range of sales activities, from prospecting to presenting to closing.

*$15.95 • 240 pages • 6 x 9-inch quality paperback • ISBN 978-0-7570-0285-4*